What a Difference a Day Makes!

'Do not boast about tomorrow, for you do not know
what a day may bring forth.'

Proverbs 27:1

WHAT A DIFFERENCE A DAY MAKES

The
Autobiography
of Brian Irvine

BRIAN IRVINE
AND STUART WEIR

MAINSTREAM
PUBLISHING

EDINBURGH AND LONDON

For the three ladies in my life:
Donna, Hannah and Christina

First published in Great Britain in 1996 by
MAINSTREAM PUBLISHING COMPANY (EDINBURGH) LTD
7 Albany Street
Edinburgh EH1 3UG

ISBN 1 85158 808 6

A catalogue record for this book is available from the British Library

Typeset in Garamond
Printed and bound in Great Britain by Butler and Tanner Ltd, Frome

CONTENTS

ACKNOWLEDGEMENTS

I am thankful for all the help that I have received throughout my career from people too numerous to list here. I hope that I have remembered to mention them all at the appropriate places in the story.

I am grateful also to all those who have contributed to this book. Thanks to everyone who took the time to respond for the 'As Others See Me' chapter, to those who supplied photographs for the book, notably Aberdeen Journals Limited, and to Helen Nunn and Katie Pollock who typed some of the manuscript. Last but not least, thanks to Stuart Weir who put together the book on the basis of many hours of conversation with me.

FOREWORD

Brian Irvine is a remarkable man. His rise to stardom and the modest way in which he has handled it is testimony to this.

Having learned his trade under Willie Miller and myself, he went on to be a rock in the Aberdeen team. Witnesses to the troubled 1994–95 season will tell you that 'Big Brian' inspired those around him not to accept defeat. Several years earlier, with great determination and willingness to learn, he had forced his way into the Scottish national team and I recall a very sound debut against a highly fancied Romanian team when a 2–1 Scottish victory helped us to the 1992 European Championship finals.

Over the years there have been a lot of characters at Aberdeen Football Club and this may account for the subtle sense of humour he has acquired. No anecdotes – read the book and judge for yourself.

I am honoured to contribute the foreword to the story of a great friend and a man who doesn't include the word 'quit' in his vocabulary.

Alex McLeish

INTRODUCTION

What a difference a day makes!

Those words sum up so well how I felt on 19 June 1995. The previous week I was flying high. We had escaped from relegation. I had been offered and had accepted a new contract. It was a relief that the season was over and I was looking forward to a nice long break before the new season. I had been speaking at a series of meetings at churches and was encouraged by these opportunities to talk about my faith.

In view of all this I was on top of the world when I approached my GP about a strange tingling feeling in my feet. Even when I was sent to Foresterhill for tests, I wasn't very bothered. I just thought he was making doubly sure that everything was okay.

A seven-day stay in hospital didn't unduly bother me, seeing as I had about six weeks before I was due back at work. Then the doctor came in and dropped the bombshell: I had multiple sclerosis. That morning I had been looking forward to getting out of hospital and having a good break with Donna and the girls. By the evening I was thinking about how to cope with a career-threatening, potentially even life-threatening illness. What a difference a day makes!

Life has been, quite literally, unbelievably good to me. At times I have struggled to believe that it was actually happening. My football career has been the fulfilment of one boyhood dream after another.

I have played in a few abandoned matches in my time but the Falkirk reserve match against Kilmarnock, abandoned after 30 minutes, saw me sign for Falkirk. If we had played on any longer and

I had made a few mistakes, I may not have got my break into senior football. What a difference a day makes!

I still thought that professional football might have passed me by however. Then came the move to the team I supported. One day I was a bank clerk; the next Alex Ferguson came to my house to meet my dad and myself and I had signed for Aberdeen. If he had not come that day it would have been Charlton for me, or perhaps not even professional football. But he signed me and allowed me the privilege of playing for the Dons over these past 12 seasons. What a difference a day makes!

On Sunday, 9 September 1990, I went to church as usual. By the time I got home from church I had been called up by Scotland. Instead of sleeping in my own bed that night, I found myself sleeping in the Marine Highland Hotel in Troon with the Scotland squad. What a difference a day makes!

The day of the penalty shoot-out in 1990 was another one that made a big difference. It started nice and calmly with breakfast for the team in our hotel and a light training session, and turned out to be an unforgettable day at Hampden with a dramatic finale, history being made with the first ever shoot-out. By the next morning I was the hero, and my photo was in all the papers. What a difference a day makes!

Another important football day was the relegation battle when we played the match against Hearts and on the same day Dundee United played against Hibs. If results had gone the other way and the late goals that we scored and United conceded had been the other way around, Aberdeen would have been relegated for the first time in the club's 93-year history. What a difference a day makes!

Other important days in my life revolve around Donna and our children, Hannah and Christina. I met my wife-to-be for the first time on a blind date. Then on 27 May 1988 I woke up single but by the end of the day I was a married man. Donna had entered my life on a permanent basis! What a difference a day makes! The birth of our children were also special days and changed our lives in major but very wonderful ways.

The day I received news of my illness is etched powerfully in my memory, and that day was very painful emotionally as well as physically. There have been many more influential days in my life and

I'm sure if you pause as you read this story you will recall many important days, some happy, some sad, which have influenced or affected your life in similar ways. Like me, you can sit back and reflect: 'What a difference a day makes!'

I hope you will find my story encouraging, challenging, interesting and enjoyable. I strongly believe that what happens to you is not as important as the way in which you handle it. My Heavenly Father knows far more than I do, and meets every need of every Christian in the way that He knows is best for us. This may not always be what we think is best, but we should trust God. He is a loving and compassionate Heavenly Father and His love – which brought Jesus to earth, to die on the cross, to rise again and make new life possible for us – has given us the choice of receiving or rejecting Jesus. If you have trust in Jesus Christ you will also be able to say 'what a difference a day makes'.

Life is uncertain and full of surprises. I had experienced my fair share of ups and downs in my career, yet nothing prepared me for the events of Monday, 19 June 1995. What a difference that day made!

1

EARLY LIFE

I was brought up in Airdrie, which is 15 miles outside of Glasgow, but my mum and dad, Bill and Isobel, were both originally from Aberdeenshire. My dad was from Logie Durno near Pitcaple and my mum from North Rayne, small villages just four miles apart and around 20 miles from Aberdeen.

I have a brother, Andrew, who is a prison officer, and a sister, Wendy, who is a nurse. I had a wonderfully happy childhood. Mum and dad made home a place where we were loved and we grew up with very good role models as examples of what a mother and father should be like. My parents always attended church and I went to the Boys' Brigade, where I was to attain the Queen's Badge award. Friday night was BB night, a great end to the school week. Saturday morning was BB football, and the afternoon was spent with the Boys' Club.

The reason my dad had moved to Airdrie in the first place was that an opportunity had come up to join the police force. He was working in Inverurie when the chief constable for Lanarkshire was having some difficulty recruiting police officers, and because he was from the North-east he centred his recruiting on Aberdeen. My dad applied, was successful and was soon on his way to Lanarkshire.

Having a father in the police force meant that I moved around a lot, to a succession of police houses. It was quite a tough environment and being the policeman's son sometimes made people want to pick on me, so I learned to look after myself. Our home in Airdrie was in a rough area but looking back, I think it was a good education for life.

Football-wise, we had a street team which played against other street teams in Airdrie, and these were always competitive games. This gave me credibility with the 'harder' team-mates in the street. Although I was quiet and not into the antics of the gangs that would cause trouble in the area, they respected this policeman's son, who was a 'nice boy' because he could play football.

My dad was a good junior footballer in his day, playing for Banks o' Dee, and he is really living out his football dreams through my career. It has always added to my enjoyment of things to be able to share them with other people and it has been a constant joy to share my football career with my dad. One thing I enjoyed doing was giving my first Scotland cap to him, just as a way of saying thanks for all that he has done for me over the years, and for the constant encouragement that he has given me, both when I was a youngster and throughout my professional career.

One of the highlights of my childhood used to be the visits to my grandad and grandma, who still lived in North Rayne. These days it is only about two and a half hours from Airdrie to Aberdeen but in those days, before the roads were improved, it could take most of the day, and the three children in the back always had ants in their pants by the time we reached Granny's.

As soon as we arrived, Andy and I would be out of the car and straight round to the local park with the football. In my dreams I was always playing for Aberdeen. I was Joe Harper or Drew Jarvie, scoring goal after goal. Never in a million years did I expect that years later I would be coached by Drew or that I would attend club functions with Joe. At that stage I was just a boy living out a dream.

A year or two back I ran a coaching course in that very same park in Logie Durno for the local kids. Its surrounding outlook is dominated by Bennachie and when the coaching was over, I remember staring at the hills for ages, with childhood memories flooding my mind. The only two teams that had ever featured in my fantasies were Aberdeen or Scotland, and the amazing thing about these dreams was that they were to become reality in later life.

If our visit coincided with an Aberdeen home game, a trip to Pittodrie really made our day. Both my parents having this strong affinity with the North-east meant that, despite living in Airdrie, my football allegiance was very definitely with Aberdeen rather than

Airdrie or one of the Glasgow teams. I took a lot of stick for this at my school, Airdrie Academy.

Andy and I played football together for St Andrew's youth club and one of the players that I often came up against in the Under-12 and Under-13 league was Peter Hetherston, later to become a team-mate at Aberdeen. At that time Andy was definitely the better player. As he grew up, however, he developed other interests, but for me it was just football, football, football. I played with my friends until it was dark. If there was no one to play with I would just go out and kick a ball around on my own.

I did well at school, gaining Highers in Maths, English, Geography and Economics and hopefully giving my teachers no problems, but it was sport that I liked best. A man called Jim McKerley was a prominent figure in my life at this time, running the school team, the Boys' Brigade and the Victoria Park team that I played for. Jim has been one of the major influences in my life. His commitment to me and all the other boys (motivated, no doubt, by his Christian faith) spoke volumes to me at the time. He was my first football manager, and was a big help to my football and in my life. Many a night, though, he must have despaired of us, considering the things we used to get up to!

I look back now with such gratitude for all that he did for me football-wise, and also for the example that he set me in life. He is a great example to all those who find themselves in positions where they are working with children. As a boy growing up I looked for and found a role model to look to. I am convinced that this can have a very positive effect on a child's adult life. As an adult working with young people you may never know the impact you will have on them, in shaping their lives ahead, but it is likely to be substantial .

One of the competitions I played in was the Airdrie Schools Cup, which has been going for almost 100 years and is one of the oldest football competitions in the world. It was a competition for primary schools but the age limit was 14, and as a result you could play in it for two years after you left primary school. I played for four years in all.

The top school in my time was Golfhill who had John McGregor playing for them, now the Rangers reserve team coach. Victoria was never one of the strongest teams in the competition but in my last year, 1979, we got to the final against Chapelhall and played at Broomfield in front of 3,000 people. We went into a 2–0 lead, but it was snatched away from us by two late goals and we lost in a penalty shoot-out. I am afraid that I missed one of the penalties. I had also missed a penalty in the quarter-final of the competition that year. The next penalty that I was to take was for Aberdeen in May 1990 but a lot of water has to go under the bridge before we come to that game!

It was real excitement for everyone at Broomfield that night, and most of our team ended up in tears. But we went back to the school canteen and celebrated our achievement in reaching the final for the first time in many years. The trophies were presented that year by Bobby Watson, who was at that time the Airdrie manager.

Other highlights of my early footballing career included winning the McKeown Cup and the Daly Cup in 1976. The following year I received the player of the year trophy from John 'Yogi' Hughes, the former Celtic and Scotland star. That year I also experienced my first football tour with Glen Thistle to the North of England in 1977.

We set off on a rainy October night in a little minibus, the 15 boys and three adults crammed into the back for the long journey south. We were singing, laughing and having a great time and when the driver announced that we had crossed the border into England, the cheer went up and *Flower of Scotland* was sung over and over again.

When I left school most of my contemporaries were considering university. Somehow I never saw this as a serious option, as after fifth year at school I felt it was time to start earning a living. My first choice was denied when I tried to join the Strathclyde Police; I got through the early interviews but failed due to my eyesight. This was a major disappointment to me, as I was keen to follow in my father's footsteps. However, had I joined the police I doubt I would have been able to progress beyond the amateur level with my football, due to the level of commitment and the shift work required by the police.

So, armed with Maths and Economics among my Highers, I applied to the Clydesdale Bank and was successful. I combined routine branch work like filing customers' cheques and making the manager's tea with more challenging studies at college on day release and at night school for my bank exams.

At this time I played for Victoria Park in the East Lothian League, and any thoughts that I might have had about playing professional football had gone. I was quite happy, working in the bank, playing for Victoria Park, watching Airdrie when I could and following Aberdeen from afar. Then, after I had been in the bank for two years, things began to happen.

I was invited for trials with Dumbarton by their manager, Billy Lamont, who was later to be my manager at Falkirk. I played four reserve games including one against Celtic reserves at Parkhead where we lost 3–1 but I scored. I also played against Airdrie reserves with my brother Andy in the team, although Andy had to be substituted at half-time with cramp. I wind him up about that to this day.

I was quite a dominant player in that league, which resulted in the chance to sign for Albion Rovers. I turned it down. I then got a trial with Falkirk, played one match and was immediately signed on provisional forms by Gregor Abel, now a scout with Aberdeen. I continued to play for Victoria Park but I was now tied to Falkirk.

At this stage I was in the habit of going out for a drink at the weekends, but when I was about 19 I stopped drinking alcohol and began to feel the benefit in my health. I felt stronger and fitter than when I had been drinking, and throughout my professional career, I have never drunk alcohol.

People sometimes ask me. 'Is it against your religion to drink?' While the Bible condemns drunkenness and drinking to excess, many Christians do drink in moderation. I have no problem with that at all. I have simply decided that for me, as a professional footballer, it is best not to drink alcohol at all.

Similarly, early on in my Aberdeen days, one of the boys in the team asked me why I didn't swear. I was not aware that I had made an impression by doing something that was natural to me, but I suppose that in a football environment swearing is 'normal'. I was just glad that the fact that I didn't swear had been noticed by my team-mates; as a Christian it comes naturally.

I played in a reserve game against Kilmarnock in February 1983 for half an hour and had a wonderful game, but then the game was abandoned due to fog. The caretaker manager, Mr Shaw, asked me into his office and asked me to sign for Falkirk, offering me wages of £7 a week. I said that I had already signed, but they couldn't find the form so I signed again! On the basis of that half-hour's play, I was signed for Falkirk.

It was clear that I was never going to get rich playing for Falkirk but that didn't matter to me. Albeit on a semi-professional basis, I had made a breakthrough into league football.

2

TO FALKIRK AND ON TO ABERDEEN

I made my league debut on 21 April 1984, for Falkirk in the Scottish First Division. It was a home game against Morton which Falkirk lost 1–0, and I found myself up against the Scottish international striker Willie Pettigrew. I didn't do badly. The *Falkirk Herald* match report stated: 'Defender Brian Irvine, making his debut for the Bairns, did a super marking job on striker Pettigrew, which indicated that he could be a player for the future.'

The Falkirk manager, Billy Lamont, was equally pleased with my contribution: 'The boy has been showing up well in the reserves. He did well in the first team against Morton. For his size, he is a very mobile player.'

I played three more games that season in the first team. At the beginning of the next season the Falkirk club captain and regular centre-half Alan Mackin was in dispute with the club and refused to re-sign. That opened the door for me to get into the first team, and I played in pre-season friendlies against Shrewsbury Town and QPR.

Playing pre-season games against teams like these was great, especially against QPR where I was up against Simon Stainrod and Clive Allen. Now, of course, I have a different perspective on pre-season friendlies and know that the game has more significance for the smaller club. The bigger club uses the game as preparation for the competitive matches ahead, and the main thing for them is to get match fitness for the start of the serious action.

This period of my life was certainly a hectic one. I was working in the Clydesdale Bank in Baillieston, just outside Glasgow, as well as studying two evenings a week for the bank professional exams. In addition I was training two nights a week at Falkirk and playing on Saturdays.

Billy Lamont was very helpful to me as I was having difficulties getting to training. I had to work late on a Thursday and was also at night school, but he made time for me to train separately with himself and Billy Simpson. As I did not have a car at that stage, he also used to give me lifts to training on the Tuesday night.

I played against Rangers at Ibrox in the League Cup where we gave a good account of ourselves, losing only 1–0 to a Dave McPherson goal late on in the game. Our league form was mixed, however and we were conceding too many goals. We lost 4–6 to Forfar and then beat Hamilton 6–4 in the next home match. At least the Brockville fans were having a feast of goals!

Early in that season I made the biggest decision of my life – to become a Christian. I had had a Christian background and had gone to church but it didn't really mean anything. It was something that you did almost out of routine. After leaving school I drifted away from church. Then one day in the car on the way to football at Falkirk, we started talking about the purpose of life. One of the others mentioned that it said in the Bible that Jesus was going to come back. Neither of my team-mates in the car that night were Christians but we had a good discussion about religion, the world and the problems of the day.

After that game I went home and I was alone. I opened up the Bible and I read from the four gospels, Matthew, Mark, Luke and John, and the Bible stories that I had read before at Sunday school, Boys' Brigade or church changed and became real. I realised that God loved me and that He had demonstrated it in such a wonderful way, by Jesus dying for me on the cross. That was the turning-point. That was the night I became a Christian.

Earlier in the day my team-mates and I had been asking, 'What has the world come to?' Now hours later I realised who had come into the world: Jesus Christ, the Son of God, my Saviour and my Lord! It was the start of a wonderful journey through this earthly life with the Lord Jesus in control.

I like this illustration to describe the Christian life. If you imagine a tandem bike, the Lord Jesus is on the front seat guiding the journey and the Christian is on the back seat. Sometimes the journey is smooth, and sometimes it is rough; sometimes it is hard and uphill, involving really hard work, and sometimes it is downhill with only light peddling involved; sometimes there is great scenery, and sometimes it is dull and drab. The weather can be beautiful, sunny and clear or it can be cold, wet and windy. Sometimes you know where you're going, sometimes you think you're completely lost; but as long as the Lord is guiding the journey, you will always be on the right path. And with trust, faith and commitment on your part, God will keep you safe on the path till the journey's end: the great Christian hope of heaven.

In my early games with Falkirk I was picking up bookings just through my enthusiasm at playing at this level of football, and I got suspended. During that suspension, Falkirk allowed me to go down to York and spend a week training with York City, where Dennis Smith and Malcolm Crosby, now manager and coach at Oxford United, were in charge. I thoroughly enjoyed that week, my first taste of full-time training. I trained with the first team and reserves and enjoyed my free time sight-seeing around York.

Mum and dad took me to Edinburgh to get the train to York. Even at 18, I wasn't used to travelling away from home by myself, and was very apprehensive. I thought that I was going to the ends of the earth as the train left Waverley Station in Edinburgh.

When I got back I immediately felt the benefit of the training and we won five of the next six games. In the period before Christmas 1985 my own form improved and I was beginning to attract attention from other teams. We had a good 3–0 win over Airdrie at Broomfield in the Scottish Cup, and I enjoyed that one as I was still living in Airdrie. Unfortunately we blew it, losing 2–1 to Forfar in the fourth round. We would have had a great chance to have reached the semis if we'd won, since Forfar played Motherwell, who at that time were in the First Division, like ourselves. They had Gary McAllister in their team, though, and Motherwell won promotion in that season, as well as reaching the semi-final of the Cup.

I held a regular place in the Falkirk team that finished third in the First Division, just missing out on promotion to the Premier

Division. In my time at Falkirk I never scored for the first team, despite now having a good record for a defender with the Dons.

My progress also resulted in an increase in pay. Billy Lamont called me into the office and said, 'You are doing really well this season and I want to increase your wages.' I was on about £7 a week and he increased it to £20 and also gave me a one-off bonus payment of £100. The funny thing was that Billy Lamont wasn't just my manager; he was, of course, also my chauffeur.

That night the £100 was bothering me and I said to Billy, 'I really appreciate the increase in my wages and the £100 but it's really too much' and I offered him £50 back. He said, 'Keep it and don't be stupid.' I don't suppose that is the way contracts and bonuses are negotiated in the English Premier League!

I nearly missed the game against Hamilton in April. I got on a train at Glasgow Queen Street station. To my horror I discovered from an announcement over the tannoy that the train's first stop was Edinburgh. I found a guard and explained my predicament. The guard said he was authorised only to stop a train in a case of emergency. We discussed whether or not playing for Falkirk could be classed as an emergency. He said that it would be quite impossible for the train to make an unscheduled stop at Falkirk for me to get off. However, he added, it sometimes happened that trains went very slowly through stations! I was able to get off and make it to Brockville for the match. I only just made it, but it ended all right as we didn't lose any goals, drawing 0–0 against Hamilton.

I was picked for the Scottish semi-professional team and played two games in Holland. We were playing a tournament with teams from Holland, Italy and England, and we beat England 3–1 and Italy 1–0. It was the first time I had ever represented Scotland at any level, and it was great to represent my country. To beat England and win the tournament really was the icing on the cake.

Also in the Scotland team was Graham Mitchell, recently of Hibs, Stevie Kirk, now of Raith Rovers, and the Celtic goalkeeper, Gordon Marshall. Terry Christie, the Stenhousemuir manager, who was in charge of the Scotland team, said to me that I would need to be ready to leave the bank and go full-time in football when we returned from the trip. I don't know if he knew something or if he was just convinced that I would get an offer from somewhere to go full-time.

I had been offered a trial with Nottingham Forest. It had been all set up that I was to play for Forest reserves against Liverpool reserves and I had arranged time off work but Forest didn't get my registration through in time so I couldn't play. However, Brian Clough still wanted to have a look at me and the plan was for me to go on an end-of-season youth tour. Unfortunately the dates clashed with the Scotland semi-professional games and I decided, patriotically, that as I had never played for Scotland I should go with the Scotland team.

Charlton Athletic were also pursuing me. I played for them in an Under-20 tournament in Turo, near Düsseldorf, playing alongside Robert Lee, now of Newcastle United and England. It was a new experience – my first ever flight in an aeroplane – and a nice birthday present for me on 24 May 1985. I was so excited that I remember telling one of the Charlton players that it was my first flight. I'd come down from Glasgow and was now off to Germany. The lad replied, 'What, twice in one day? You're taking a bit of a risk aren't you?'

Lennie Lawrence, the Charlton manager, met me after the tournament and said that he wanted to sign me. I said that I was interested but that I had to speak to Falkirk first, as I was under contract to them.

During the close season Charlton Athletic maintained their interest in me. With the uncertainty going on for several months I spoke with my minister in Airdrie one night after I returned from the Scotland trip. He gave me good practical advice at that time and at the end of our chat we prayed about my future, for guidance and that God would open or close doors according to His own will. A couple of weeks later, on returning from holiday, it seemed too good to be true that Aberdeen were now in the picture.

What happened was that I went on holiday to Torquay, and on the way back I met Lennie Lawrence in a hotel in Bristol. He was so convinced that I would sign that he had brought his secretary – plus a typewriter – to type out the contract for me to sign.

While waiting at the hotel for the meeting, I rang Falkirk to tell the manager that I had arrived at the hotel. Billy Lamont then told me that Aberdeen had made an offer for me. I was delighted. If I could have chosen a club I wanted to play for, it would have been Aberdeen.

Now if Real Madrid or Inter Milan had made an offer for me I could not have been more excited. Lennie Lawrence had said to me,

'If you sign for Charlton I will put you straight into the first team. If you sign for a bigger club, you won't get first-team football so soon.' I knew that at Aberdeen with Willie Miller and Alex McLeish, the two best centre-halfs in Scotland, I could not expect to get into the first team straightaway. However, Aberdeen was my team; the team I supported and the team I dreamed of playing for.

Charlton offered me three times the signing-on fee that Aberdeen did and a higher wage without any negotiation from me. I told Lennie that I would let him know in a few days. The following Monday Alex Ferguson came down to Airdrie to see me. To have his Mercedes parked outside the house was a real talking-point for the neighbours!

I signed for Aberdeen the following day at Dunblane Hydro, with Billy Lamont, the Aberdeen manager, and Willie Garner who was assistant manager at Aberdeen. The fee was £55,000, plus £25,000 when I played so many games for Aberdeen and £30,000 when I won my first Scotland cap – £110,000 in total.

Aberdeen's offer was £5,000 to sign on and £230 a week. They could have said that I had to give them £5,000 and I would have agreed, so keen was I to sign for Aberdeen! In fact I signed a blank contract and trusted them to fill in the details. I just felt that if the manager of the top team in Scotland was offering me the chance to become a full-time professional footballer, I certainly wasn't going to fall out with him over the details. I thought it was a three-year contract but when it was filled in by the club secretary I discovered it was for four years – but I didn't mind! In fact, it was even better that it was four years.

I signed for the Dons in July 1985 as 'one for the future' in the shadow of the club's other big signing that summer, Jim Bett, who was to become a good football friend to me in the years ahead. Jim may have appeared quite serious to the fans but he was full of good banter in the dressing-room throughout his time at Pittodrie.

There was a certain irony in the timing. I had slogged away for three years at night school on my banking exams, spurred on by the knowledge that promotion to a higher level in the bank would follow. I passed the exams in the summer of 1985. The next thing I did was to resign from the bank to become a full-time professional footballer.

But my colleagues in the bank were always great to me. As a part-time footballer, I was a bit different and, from the manager down, everyone in the branch was always so helpful to me that it was sad to leave in some ways. Yet, despite the step into the unknown that I was taking, it was great to be leaving for the exciting challenge of trying to make it as a full-time player with the Dons.

3

BECOMING AN ABERDEEN PLAYER

When I first signed for Aberdeen, I remember being in the dressing-room with all my heroes, all of whom were household names. It was as if I had won a competition to train with Aberdeen for a week!

At that stage Aberdeen had just won the league two years in a row (1983–84 and 1984–85), and had won the Scottish Cup three years running. The team had won the European Cup Winners' Cup in 1983 and had reached the semi-final the following season.

One day I was a part-time footballer and a bank clerk. The next day I was a player with the best team in Scotland. One day if you had asked me who my manager was, I would have said Mr Young, the manager of the Clydesdale Bank where I worked. The next day, my manager was Alex Ferguson. What a difference a day makes! For me being introduced to the top level for the first time, I could not have asked for a better manager, although at first I was probably too much in awe of him.

When I moved up to Aberdeen the family connection was a big help. For the first month I stayed in digs in the city centre then I moved out to stay with my aunt and uncle, Frank and June Duguid, at Kintore and stayed there for three years. At that time I did not have a car. The only problem was that my aunt and uncle's house was about a mile and a half from the main road.

At first I went to Kintore Parish Church. The church had a Boys' Brigade company and since I had been helped so much by the BB, I wanted to give something back, so I became an officer in the BB at Kintore.

Another memory of that period was a man called Donald Smith who became quite an inspiration to me. He was a retired Church of Scotland minister, who had been held as a prisoner of war by the Japanese. Often after training I used to go to visit him and just sit and listen to his stories. I can still remember so much of what he told me, both the stories and all the wise advice he gave to me. Sometimes I would go to see him on a Friday and it was as good as a team-talk inspiring me for the next day.

My journey to training was by bike to the road, then bus to Kittybrewster. However, there was no direct bus from that side of Aberdeen to Pittodrie so I started to walk. Later Jim Leighton used to pick me up at Kittybrewster. One day, after all the effort of getting to training, I fell asleep on the way home and was awakened by the conductor at the end of the line, ten miles beyond Kintore where I should have got off the bus. I then had to wait for the next bus into Aberdeen. That was the last time I ever went to sleep on the bus!

In fact that acted as an incentive for me and quite soon afterwards I passed my driving test and got a car. Uncle Frank and Aunt June gave me a great environment to try to establish myself at Aberdeen. It was like being at home and I didn't suffer the problems with homesickness which other young boys have, coming to Aberdeen from Glasgow or the south.

Frank and I would talk football for hours in the evenings. Aunt June would feed me up – too well, in fact, as I was nearly 15 stone at this point! I had three great years with Frank and June, staying there till 27 May 1988, and I only left them because I was getting married that same day!

My introduction to full-time football was during pre-season training, which as I describe elsewhere was particularly tough under Archie Knox. I still remember going home terrified about what was to come the next day. Running up the dreaded Seaton Hill was part of pre-season for several years, and a part that we all feared. Pre-season nowadays is more sophisticated and the achilles injuries Seaton Hill used to cause made it history – a pre-season horror story.

That season was all about learning. I played in the reserve team that finished runners-up in the reserve league. Such was the strength of the squad that the Aberdeen reserve team could certainly have held its own with quite a number of other clubs' first teams. There were experienced players like Billy Stark in the team as well as young players who were still to make their name at Aberdeen, like Brian Grant. Brian has spent his career at Pittodrie like myself and I am pleased to see he has enjoyed his testimonial year. He is a quiet unassuming guy who likes to do his talking with his boots, which is fine on the football pitch but a bit strange when, for example, he's out for a meal with friends! We have been able to encourage each other through the various stages of our careers as they have occurred at similar times. I look on Brian as a good friend and hope he feels the same way about me.

Billy Stark, John McMaster and Peter Weir were three players who really looked after me in my early days in Aberdeen. I keep in touch with them to this day. For 11 years I have changed next to Stewart McKimmie. When I was first in Aberdeen Stewart invited me to his house for meals on many occasions, which was something that really helped me to settle. Louise and Stewart were newly married when I arrived and I'll never forget their hospitality to me at that crucial stage of my life.

I played nine games for Aberdeen in that season. The first two were pre-season friendlies in Switzerland. I came on as sub at half-time against Schauffeusen when we won 2–1 and played the whole game against Lausanne when we won 6–2 and I scored a goal. It was Willie Miller's 699th game for Aberdeen, beating Bobby Clark's record. It was my first visit to Switzerland and the Alpine scenery was breathtaking.

My other first team appearances were friendlies and testimonial games against Meadowbank, Inverness Caley, Clyde, Dunfermline, Brechin and Arbroath. I also played in a world youth tournament (Under-20) in Viareggio, Italy, and in a five-a-side tournament at Wembley where we lost to Arsenal in the second round.

I was lined up for a competitive debut against Montrose in January, but the game was postponed and the delay gave everyone a chance to get fit. The season finished on a high, though, with my league debut against Clydebank on 3 May when we won 6–0. The Aberdeen team was Gunn, McKimmie, MacQueen, Stark, Irvine, McIntyre, Gray, Hewitt, MacDougall, McMaster, Weir.

The season was successful, with Aberdeen winning the Skol Cup and the Scottish Cup. I was in the squad for the cup final even though I was never going to play. I was also included in the squad for the European Cup match with Servette of Switzerland. It was an indication of the progress I had made during that first season.

I was not expecting much from my first season. In fact, I would have been quite content just to learn the Aberdeen way in the reserves and adapt to full-time training. The opportunities that came my way were therefore a real bonus. The final fortnight of the season was tremendous: after making my league debut it was unbelievable to be part of the squad for the Scottish Cup final, and the season ended too soon for me.

The 1986–87 season saw me break through to the fringe of the first team. I was in the starting line-up in 19 league games and scored my first goal for the first team in a competitive match. Overall it was a disappointing season for Aberdeen, particularly after the previous seasons' successes. We finished fourth in the league, lost on penalties to Celtic in the quarter-final of the Skol Cup and again to Celtic in the third round of the Scottish Cup after two replays.

The season could not have started better for me. I played three matches on a pre-season tour to Sweden. Neale Cooper's departure and an injury to Willie gave me my chance. Willie had picked up an injury in the World Cup and missed the first three games.

On that tour I found myself caught by a practical joke. I was needing a haircut and Billy Stark, I was told, used to be a hairdresser. He actually convinced me that he used to work for Vidal Sassoon whilst playing for St Mirren! I thought this must be true since Billy always had a well-groomed head of hair himself. I only became suspicious when, one by one, the boys came to view the haircutting, including Alex Ferguson and Archie Knox. Needless to say, the finished result was none too flattering!

I also played in a pre-season friendly against Stuttgart at Pittodrie, playing against Jurgen Klinsmann. Then when the season proper got under way, Willie was still injured. Even when he returned to the team I held my place, moving to left-back. At Falkirk I had only ever played in the centre but at Aberdeen, with Willie and Alex automatic choices for centre when fit, I was called upon to play at both right and left-back that season.

32

In fact I played the first nine games of the season, comprising league games against Dundee United, Hibernian, Hamilton, Celtic, Dundee, St Mirren and Hearts as well as Skol Cup ties against Alloa and Clyde. In the game against Hamilton, Jim Leighton received a very nasty blow to the face and had to go off – fortunately it didn't spoil his good looks. Archie Knox came on and asked for volunteers to go in goal and I said I would. I played the last 15 minutes in goal and caught a couple of crosses, keeping a clean sheet. When I got home to Kintore Frank had put up a notice on the garage door saying, 'Parking only for Aberdeen's new Jim Leighton'. And as the Aberdeen matchday magazine, *The Don*, put it, 'You can bet no other player has deputised for Willie Miller and Jim Leighton in the same match.'

The next week was against Celtic at Parkhead with a crowd of 46,000. It was the biggest game I had ever played in. I also made my European debut in October 1986, away to Sion of Switzerland. The atmosphere was really special, but unfortunately Aberdeen lost 3–0. We conceded two early goals, the first when Stewart McKimmie sliced the ball into his own goal from a corner, and we were eliminated from the competition. The Aberdeen team that had won the Cup Winners' Cup in 1983 had beaten Sion 11–1, and here we were two years later losing to them 4–2 on aggregate.

Even though we lost, however, I remember thinking before the game, 'I am playing in a European Cup game; this is every schoolboy's dream!' At this stage of my career I was on a steep learning curve going through a succession of 'firsts'. While defeat is not what you are looking for, I have found throughout my career that you often learn more from defeat than you do from victory.

In November 1986 there was a change of manager. The reserves and youth players were training at Seaton Park with Archie Knox in charge, when Alex Ferguson's Mercedes approached at high speed. He was shouting for Archie. Archie got in and they drove off, leaving us on our own. We organised a game among ourselves and after about an hour the bus, driven by Teddy Scott, came to take us back to Pittodrie.

We were all wondering what was so important that Archie had to go off without any explanation. That night it was announced that Alex Ferguson was the new manager of Manchester United with

Archie Knox as his assistant. That was the last we saw of Alex. Archie stayed for a week and then joined Alex in Manchester. Ian Porterfield was the new manager.

In my early days in Aberdeen, I was living in the middle of nowhere. My life revolved around football and church, with girls not really figuring in my priorities. The fact that the congregation at the Kintore church, my main circle of friends, was largely elderly, meant that I did not even meet many girls of my own age.

Tommy McIntyre, who now plays for Airdrie, was at that stage at Aberdeen and, like me, playing mainly in the reserves. He knew that I was a Christian. At that time he was going out with a girl who was an air hostess with Air UK. That girl had a friend called Donna Main who had just become a Christian and seemed awfully excited about it. In fact she was going to be baptised at the Deeside Christian Fellowship and had told her friend all about it.

Tommy and his girlfriend came up with the idea of linking Donna and me, and a blind date was arranged. Tommy gave me Donna's phone number so I rang her, and was greeted by an awfully polite Aberdeen voice. We arranged to meet on the Thursday night. However, as Thursday night was my BB night I couldn't meet Donna until 9 p.m.

I put on what I thought were quite trendy clothes but which Donna later told me was more an uncoordinated mess. Tommy had said to me that Donna quite liked junk food so I decided I would take her to Pizzaland. When I rang her doorbell I was greeted by someone who was all dressed up and beautifully coordinated, expecting to be taken to Gerrard's or somewhere similar. While Donna is comfortable with junk food when the occasion demands it, on this occasion she was expecting something a bit better!

For me it was love at first sight. I could not believe that such a beautiful girl was really going to go out with me. Donna later told me that she was at the same time wondering what she had let herself in for and was feeling distinctly unsure about it.

There are two things I remember most about that first date. First is how lucky I was to finish up on a blind date with such a beautiful girl. Second was how openly and enthusiastically Donna spoke about her new Christian faith and her baptism. That might surprise people who know me as someone who speaks openly and publicly about my

Christian faith. But you need to realise that at that time, when I was going to Kintore Parish Church, to hear someone speak so openly and with such enthusiasm about her faith was new to me.

That first date was in November 1986, and we were engaged the following October and married in May 1988. Perhaps the most surprising thing about my relationship with Donna was that, given the impression I made on the first date, I ever got a second one! Of course I didn't know any of this at the time. In fact, I had thoroughly enjoyed the date, and Donna had won my heart. She managed to conceal all her initial reservations, and the relationship developed from there.

The first game I played under Ian Porterfield was at home to Hearts on 21 January 1987. It proved to be a memorable game for all the wrong reasons. I played well but got a blow in the eye and finished up in hospital for five days, having to keep my eye as still as possible to stop the bleeding behind it. This was how I made an impression on the new manager!

I was out for a month with the injury but I had made progress and had won his confidence. He looked after me contract-wise. I was still on the contract that I had signed when I joined Aberdeen from Falkirk, but now that I was playing for the first team, the money I was on was less than most of the other players and Ian Porterfield gave me a new contract. He followed the same pattern as Billy Lamont did in encouraging me and I appreciated that from him.

I finished that season well with a run of ten games in the first team and I scored three goals, one each against Celtic, Clydebank and Rangers. It is funny how you seem to score against certain teams. Celtic would be one of my teams. I remember my first goal against Celtic in March 1987. Tommy Burns gave me a really bad tackle and left me with stud marks down my leg. I remember that the tackle wound me up and made me more determined, so when I was up for a free-kick, sheer determination took me to the ball. It almost needed an extension to my neck to get there, but I made it.

I have a picture from the newspaper of that goal and the funny thing is that the nearest Celtic player to me when I scored was Roy Aitken. Now I wonder what happened to him and where he finished up! Another thing about that goal was that it was the day of my parents' 25th wedding anniversary and there was a party for the family that night. That I had scored in such a big match was a big thrill for everyone at the family celebration in Inverurie.

Ian Porterfield often played me in midfield in a man-marking role. One game I particularly remember is the last game of the 1986–87 season, against Rangers on 2 May. Rangers had to win to clinch the league title, although in the end Celtic lost so it didn't matter. Terry Butcher scored to put Rangers ahead.

I was marking Graeme Souness. Four minutes into the game Souness caught me on the knee with a horizontal challenge and after 25 minutes he did it again and was sent off. I remember praying beforehand about the game as I felt that there was no way I was going to be able to contain him. I felt it was a 'David and Goliath' situation in terms of skill, experience and standing in the game. But as it turned out he pressed the self-destruct button and was shown the red card.

Late in the game we got a corner which was only half cleared, and I got in front of Graham Roberts to drive it home. It was the end of the season, and at the end the crowd streamed on and took the posts down.

The Rangers game was a milestone in another way: accompanied by Doug and Bruce Smith, it was the first football match that Donna had ever attended. It was an eventful afternoon with me scoring, Graeme Souness being sent off, Rangers winning the league and a pitch invasion. At the end of the game, Bruce turned to Donna and said, 'That was a cracking game. You couldn't have asked for a more exciting first match.' Donna replied, 'Really? I found it quite boring!' Donna has always supported me in my career, but I have to recognise that football will never be one of her great passions.

Overall it was a good season for me. With Alex and Willie around I was not going to be a first choice but I had managed to play a reasonable number of games. In fact, apart from numbers 9 and 11, I played in every position for Aberdeen. To finish with goals against both the Old Firm was the icing on the cake. *The Don* commented: 'It is an interesting statistic . . . that the Dons may have signed a new Ian Rush. Aberdeen have never lost when Irvine has scored!'

At the end of that season, six months into my relationship with Donna, I went to Puerto Pollensa in Majorca, with Donna and her mum – my future mother-in-law! I was in one room and they were in the other. As Christians, something we were totally committed to was keeping our relationship pure sexually until we were married and committed to each other before God. I believe that it is a very important Christian principle to obey, particularly with so many in the world today not doing so. It is a principle that Christians need to be reminded of, and we should not be afraid of being laughed at for following the teaching of the Bible. I believe that God provided sex for our enjoyment, but only within marriage, because sex outside of marriage is wrong.

4

EARLY YEARS AT ABERDEEN (1987–89)

The 1987–88 season left Aberdeen finishing fourth in the league and winning none of the cups. The lack of success ultimately cost Ian Porterfield his job. However, it also illustrates what a thin line there is between success and failure. Aberdeen lost the Skol Cup final on penalties. In the Scottish Cup we went out to Dundee United 1–0 after extra time in the second replay, and in Europe it was on away goals. Had we won those three, the season could have been so different and Ian Porterfield's job secure. But then that's football.

The season started well with a pre-season tour of Wales and the South-west of England with games against Newport County, Dawlish Town, Plymouth Argyle and Exeter City. Jimmy Mullen and Ian Porterfield were a bit more relaxed than were both previous and later managers. During our trip to Dawlish we were given more free time than normal – in the evenings! Normally in pre-season training camps we are supposed to rest during the evening and have an early night. However, several nights out were permitted and instead of being given a 'normal' curfew this time we weren't allowed in till after midnight!

The domestic season saw me playing league games against Rangers, Motherwell, Dundee United, Falkirk, Celtic, Hibs and Hearts. We had a good run in the Skol Cup, and I scored my first goal of the season as we beat Brechin 5–1. I also played in the quarter-final when we beat Celtic 1–0 at Pittodrie.

That set us up for a local derby semi-final against Dundee at Tannadice, and we had a great start when Bobby Connor scored. I was playing in midfield and marking John Brown, now of Rangers, and I was able to get a second goal before half-time. I had the great thrill of hearing the crowd chanting my name in that game. The following day, 24 September 1987, Donna and I got engaged.

I lost my place in the team between the semi-final and final of the Skol Cup. I was expecting to be on the bench for the final but unfortunately that didn't happen either. For the first time – but not the last – I watched a big game from the stand. We met Rangers in the final and played really well, but after finishing 3–3 we lost 5–3 on penalties.

I didn't play for the first team for nearly three months with the exception of a European tie against Feyenoord. I was brought in to play in the away leg when Stewart McKimmie was suspended, and we were 2–1 up from the first leg. I cleared a ball which unfortunately went to one of their players and was eventually crossed in for their equaliser. We lost on away goals.

I was a bit surprised the next day when one paper headline started 'Irvine blunder cost the Dons'. I was quite upset because I didn't believe I was directly involved in their goal. That was my first taste of how the opinion of one journalist could influence public opinion back home.

My return to league football came early in 1988 when Alex McLeish got injured just before the Hibs game in January. Charlie Nicholas had just signed for us, and Ian Porterfield took the team away for a mid-season break to Torremolinos.

On that trip I was rooming with Stewart. There was one incident that still makes me laugh. At one point Stewart had to rush to the toilet to be sick, and while doing so, his false tooth came out and was flushed down the loo before he realized what had happened. Louise McKimmie was not very sympathetic towards her toothless husband on his return home.

Another important event around that time for me personally was my baptism. Deeside Christian Fellowship (DCF) is an independent evangelical church which has been a real help to me in my Christian life. Despite living about 15 minutes drive from Deeside, we are really at home there amongst Christian friends. The pastor, Tom Lawson, and the leaders have been particularly supportive of me in my football career and the late Jim Gill, like Bruce Smith, was one of a handful of role models I have had in my life. The church has continued to grow since its beginning in September 1977 and I am so thankful to God for my involvement there.

DCF does not baptise babies. Baptism, involving full immersion in a tank of water, is for adults who have made a personal decision to become a Christian. It was something that I had not yet done, but it had often been in my mind. On 3 January 1988 I finally did it. That public acknowledgement of my Christian faith was a significant point in my Christian life.

Our next match was against Dunfermline at Pittodrie and the ground was packed because it was Charlie Nicholas's home debut. The reports back home from Torremolinos were of Charlie looking good in training. The only place Charlie – or the rest of the team for that matter – was looking good on that trip was in the Spanish bars. We were given the whole trip off training, except one session in the rain in the hotel car park, much to the amusement of the locals.

Charlie wasn't really fit to begin with, having come from Arsenal reserves. The touches were there but he didn't make a great contribution overall. Yet his charisma had an effect on players and fans alike from that game on, and he did a great job for Aberdeen. I was sad to see him leave.

When Alex was fit again I dropped out. At that stage of my career I had to be happy just to pick up appearances when I could. In the end I played 17 league games plus five cup games that season. A highlight was getting the only goal of the game against Rangers at Ibrox on 30 April as we won 1–0. Graham Roberts didn't get the ball properly cleared and I picked it up and shot home. That proved to be Graham Roberts's last game for Rangers. Apparently he and the manager, Graeme Souness, had such a row about the goal after the game that he never played for Rangers again.

I think that in terms of ability I am a pretty ordinary player. What is extraordinary about me is my commitment and passion, not only for the game, but for Aberdeen Football Club. That commitment and passion has helped an ordinary player to have a long and successful career with that one club, and it helped me a lot at this stage when I was in and out of the team.

41

I have often been asked how I coped with being on the fringe of the first team. The answer is that I got used to it but I never accepted it. Over the first four seasons at Aberdeen there was an improvement and each season I played more games. My faith helped me to have patience and to accept that there was a purpose, and although things didn't happen in the way I might have wanted them to I knew that everything was in God's hands and God was in control.

Being sub is a funny role. You can sit there for 90 minutes and not come on. Equally someone can get injured at any time and you can come on at any stage of the game. Either way you have got to be ready if needed.

I have always been pretty fit and have always had good stamina. Over the years, all the endless hours of practice beginning when I was a boy developed what natural skill and ability that I had. Even as a professional I used to stay behind at the end of training to practise with the ball and work on certain things. In giving advice to any young player, I can not emphasise enough the importance of even an extra ten minutes on a regular basis to improve your game – whether just kicking the ball against a wall to improve your touch, dribbling through cones or working on heading in twos.

I would say to any player whose weakness is passing, get a friend and a bag of balls and just practise passing, controlling and passing back to each other. On most days training is only for two hours, so there is plenty of time to do a little extra. If you are in the first team and playing once or twice a week, it is important not to overdo it. However, for a young player who is trying to break through, an extra session in the afternoon can sometimes really pay dividends.

Talking of my own ball skills, I have been the butt of one or two jokes concerning such matters. I was once among a group of players who went to see the comedian Tony Roper at the Capitol Theatre in Aberdeen. Tony revealed an exclusive from the stage: Adidas were claiming that their new 'Predator' boots were so good that they could even make Brian Irvine kick straight! The next day when I was in for training I found that Eoin Jess, who wears Predators, had left a pair at my place in the changing-room.

This was not the only time I was on the wrong end of Tony's humour. He also used to tell a story about Craig Brown complaining that it was very difficult to be Scotland team manager: he'd had 57 players cry off through injury and unfortunately not one of them was Brian Irvine!

As a player I look on myself as a good defender. My job is to win the ball and pass it or lay it off to a team-mate. I try to play simply, with no tricks, and let our midfield players take over. I think I am best when concentrating on doing my own job of winning the ball – in the air or on the ground – and then, providing I can do it without putting a team-mate in trouble, giving it to someone who can perhaps use his greater skill on the ball to set something up. I can't do what Brian Laudrup does with a ball but there are other ways to make a contribution to the team.

My ambition was always to be the best defender, not necessarily the best player. To be a great defender, you don't have to be able to do ball-juggling tricks. The crowd always likes a defender who is comfortable on the ball, and who likes to take the ball down, beat a man and go forward. However, that kind of player is also likely to cost his team goals by being caught in possession.

That is something that I haven't ever really done, although occasionally I have a rush of blood to the head, and try it! The midfield and attacking players are the ones with the skills to run at people and so on. Being part of the team means doing your own job. My job is to mark a forward, keeping tight to him, and to keep in a good position, win headers, and win tackles. It is often so simple that no one notices it. Good defending is often nipping an attack in the bud.

Sometimes Aberdeen score a goal from a move which I started. The opposition is in possession, I win the ball, slip it to Gary Smith, Eoin Jess makes a great run and eventually Scott Booth scores with a great shot. My part was perhaps just getting a small touch on the ball. Everybody remembers Scott's shot but nobody remembers my part, yet, for the team, my tackle was vital. It is simple things like that that I am working on, as well as keeping my concentration so as to be alert when I am needed.

I am the type of player who needs confidence. To be confident I need to be given encouragement, and I have always responded well to managers who do so. If your confidence gets a knock, your play is likely to suffer.

Because of my experience I am now good at reading the game and at being in the right position. I am constantly looking across the pitch as well as up and down it, to check that the back four are working as a unit and that I am in the right position in relation to Stewart and Gary or whoever is in the team. Forwards can play clever balls all day, but if the defence is right positionally, you can make it very difficult for them to find the space to create anything.

In my early days I was probably happiest when I had someone to mark. For example, under Ian Porterfield I was sometimes given a midfield marking role which I found an easy role to play. You only had one thing to concentrate on; a specific job to do without having to worry about positioning. The last player I had to man-mark was Ruud Gullit in the Scotland–Holland game, but I couldn't really claim to have kept him out of the game completely. Latterly at Aberdeen we have played in zones. You are just responsible for your zone and if a forward moves out of your zone, you just pass him on to your team-mate.

Going back to the 1987–88 season, there is one important event to report. Donna and I got married on 27 May 1988. The wedding was at Deeside Christian Fellowship in Milltimber, and Bruce Smith conducted the ceremony. This was very appropriate as Jenny Smith, Bruce's wife, had quite a big role to play in Donna's early Christian life. From the time that Donna and I started going out together, Bruce and Jenny took a real interest in us and it was through Bruce that I met his brother, Douglas, and his wife, Susan, who were to become close friends.

On the subject of Deeside Christian Fellowship, I would like to record my appreciation of all the help and support that so many people at the church have given me over the years, both spiritually and in terms of the interest they have taken in my football. Whenever I have played in important matches for Aberdeen or Scotland, there have always been several faxes from people in the church to encourage me on the day.

Sporting activities that the church itself is involved in include a golf day where church members bring friends who are not church-goers, so giving them the opportunity to meet Christians. They play a round of golf together and hear a little message from a speaker. It is a good example of taking the church to people who don't attend church, and hopefully breaking down some of the barriers and preconceptions of what Christians are like. For the children, the church runs football coaching weeks during the school holidays and also encourages the parents to come along to watch.

There are about 12 members of the church who have a block of season tickets in the front row at Pittodrie. Their prayers for me have really helped throughout the ups and downs of my career. As I become more and more in the public eye, the encouragement I get from them has been a real boost.

Now Donna has absolutely no understanding of football, yet she has had quite an impact on my career. Peter Weir and Billy Stark both told me that they saw a different – and better – attitude in me to training after I met Donna.

This is a wonderful opportunity to thank Donna publicly for her love and support for me over the years. She gave up her work as an air hostess in 1990 to have Hannah, and then Christina arrived in 1994. Donna and I are from different backgrounds. She was brought up in the west end of Aberdeen, with her dad, Donald, running the family fish business until he retired and her mum, Irene, being involved in the fashion business, whereas I was brought up in several council estates in Airdrie. There was, therefore, a big contrast in terms of the environment we were used to in our early years.

It has been difficult for Donna to be stuck at home so often and the worst period was after Christina's birth, when she wouldn't sleep through the night and Donna was suffering from chronic tiredness. Donald and Irene were great and helped to look after Hannah and Christina, and now when I am away overnight, preparing for an away match, I know that Donna and the girls are being well looked after.

She has also had to accept many times the sacrifices involved in being a footballer's wife. I've lost count of the number of weddings and other social events Donna has gone to alone, because they were on a Friday or a Saturday.

People often have an image of footballers as people who enjoy a full social life. Our experience has been the opposite, with many missed opportunities to enjoy our friends' company. If you think about it, most social engagements are on a Friday or Saturday night. I can never go on a Friday and not on a Saturday if we have an away game. My social life is pretty limited during the season.

It is also a very typical situation that when we meet people, they will unwittingly ask me about my football and don't give much attention to Donna and her interests. This is a situation which footballers' wives often encounter, but it makes it no easier to handle.

During the 'relegation' year, things were difficult for us at home. Donna was tired, I was unsure of our future and of the club's future and the stress and strain took its toll on our relationship. I was wrong to take my problems home and it is a true saying that 'we spend our lives being nice to people we don't really know and often hurt the ones we love the most'.

But we committed ourselves before God – and for better or for worse, whatever the stage of your relationship, you have to remember the love that led to your making such a commitment. Today, with marriage break-up on the increase, there is a trend of simply walking away from a difficult period in a marriage. Communication is so important if you want to avoid this, and trusting and respecting each other again is a vital ingredient.

The first five years after getting married were the best years of my career, and I believe this was a reflection of the happiness and stability that Donna had brought into my life. It is amazing how much your home life affects your football. Your form can easily dip around the time of the birth of a baby, for instance, because of the change that brings to your life.

The 1988–89 season saw me make more progress. I played in 27 league games, my highest total so far. I was, however, still basically an understudy to Willie and Alex. At the end of the 1988 season, Ian Porterfield resigned and was replaced by Alex Smith and Jocky Scott.

That year we went to Holland for a pre-season tournament with Feyenoord, Real Madrid and Antwerp. We lost 2–1 to Feyenoord in a game where Willie Miller was caught by a late tackle after 35 minutes and I came on as a sub. I also played in the game against Antwerp which finished 0–0. It was a great experience for me at that stage of my career to be playing against these top teams in Europe, especially as the games attracted crowds of 30,000 people in Feyenoord's impressive stadium.

That moment in the Feyenoord game was more significant than we realised at the time. The injury to Willie's knee was the beginning of the knee trouble which dogged him for the rest of his career. While Willie made a quick recovery from the injury at the time, the problem was always there in the background.

As the Scottish season started, it was Alex and Willie who were playing together at the heart of the defence. I was regularly on the bench, coming on at right-back, in midfield or wherever. Again it was a step in the right direction, for while the bench is not ideal, it certainly beats sitting in the stand! Even when I was playing the papers would often say that the team was missing Willie. I always had to tell myself not to take it personally but to recognise that Willie had such a great influence on the team. At this point I had still played fewer games for Aberdeen than Willie had Scottish caps!

I had to accept that when they were fit, Willie and Alex were the automatic first choices and to acknowledge that they were playing together as well as ever. I could only give my best and push them as hard as possible, then take my chances when they came along. I tried to look on it as the apprenticeship I had missed out on by not coming into football straight from school. I felt that I was learning things that would be of use to me in the future.

One of the games where I came on as sub was in Dresden in the UEFA Cup. The match was played in front of 36,000 people, and there was quite a hostile atmosphere. I came on at right-back but finished up at centre-forward. The first leg at Pittodrie had finished 0–0, so it was always going to be tough, but then Davie Robertson was sent off and our chances really went. We lost 2–0.

The next week, 8 October, I came on as sub against Rangers in the game best remembered for the infamous tackle by Neil Simpson on Ian Durrant. It was a very unfortunate incident which the Rangers fans always seem to bring up every time Rangers play Aberdeen. That day I came on at 1–1 and we went on to win 2–1, with Charlie Nicholas getting the winner after Jim Bett's penalty.

I was again on the bench for the Skol Cup final against Rangers, played in front of 72,000 people, coming on towards the end. We lost 3–2 with two goals from Davie Dodds not enough to get our hands on the trophy.

Willie was increasingly struggling with his knee that season, despite having surgery. His misfortune gave me more opportunities in first-team football. I had a good spell towards the middle of the season, playing nine games in a row (between December and February,) and also played the last six of the season, finishing with 21 starts and six sub appearances in the league.

Other memories from that season include the epic Scottish Cup fourth round ties with Dundee United, the second replay going to extra time before Mixu Paatelainen scored to win the tie. I played in all three games. I scored two goals that season, against St Mirren and Hearts, and the header against Hearts was possibly my best goal for the club so far.

In February we went to Germany for a five-a-side tournament during the German mid-season break. We flew over to Hanover and we were delayed on the journey, so we literally turned up just in time to play. We enjoyed the experience of playing in the tournament although we were never going to win. We gave a good account of ourselves and it was a nice break from our usual routine, but we were a bit lacking in the techniques of five-a-side perhaps compared to some of the European sides.

By the end of the 1988–89 season I had been at Aberdeen for four years. I had played over 60 league games, and I had come on as sub during the Skol Cup final at Hampden. I had sampled European football. I was a valuable member of the squad but had not quite managed to pin down a regular first-team place. Perhaps that was round the next corner.

5

CUP FINAL DRAMA

The 1989–90 season proved to be the most successful one for Aberdeen since the days of Alex Ferguson. We were second in the league and won the two cups. I played 31 out of 36 league games – 28 starts and three appearances as sub – including starting 25 games in a row from November.

Again we started with a pre-season visit to Holland. We played in a tournament in Lemmer followed by a friendly in Utrecht, where I was later to play for Scotland. In Holland, I asked the manager if I could go to church on the Sunday morning. He said that there would be no problem with that. He added, 'There are a few of the other players who could do with going to church, do you think you could take them too?' It was the Church of Scotland in Rotterdam and it could have been the Church of Scotland in Kintore. It was really just like home.

Again from the start of that season I was always involved. If I wasn't in the starting line-up I'd be on the bench. I was called into the team for the away leg of the Rapid Vienna UEFA Cup tie, where we lost 1–0 to a Jan-Aage Fjortoft goal and went out of the competition on away goals. The match was played in a great stadium but in a very hostile environment. The Rapid team were also very cynical. They were a very capable and skilful side but even in the home leg their approach was very negative, with time-wasting and constant niggles and intimidation. Playing in Europe really is the pinnacle of club football so it was great to be involved, but to come so close only to go out on away goals was hard to bear.

We had a good Skol Cup run, beating Albion Rovers 2–0 away, and my home town team, Airdrieonians, 4–0 at Pittodrie. We beat St Mirren in the quarter-final and Celtic in the semi-final, but I did not play in either of those games.

I was on the bench for the final against Rangers. It was 1–1 after 90 minutes, then Paul Mason scored his second goal and the winner for us in extra time. Eoin Jess was playing at the age of 17 and I replaced him with five minutes of extra time left, just to help keep it tight as we held on to our 2–1 lead. I can't say I made a great contribution to the game but I still really felt part of it. Being on the pitch at the final whistle, being part of the presentation of the cup and the lap of honour and knowing that I had helped bring another trophy to Aberdeen made me feel part of a successful team.

It was my first winner's medal, although I had played in the 1988 final when we lost. The difference between winning and losing is phenomenal. If you lose you go up and get your medal and then into the dressing-room, get changed and it is just another game. Being on the park as a winner when the final whistle blew was a great moment.

Willie's continuing injury problems brought me back into the first team. It was about that time that Aberdeen signed Hans Gillhaus from PSV Eindhoven for £650,000. He was such an exciting player, fast and skilful, and he gave everyone such a buzz when he was on the ball. He was like a world-beater early on, and his impact in that first season was immense.

His first game was against Dunfermline. We won 3–0 and Hans scored two goals, both of which I set up with headers back across the goal. He put them in, first with a spectacular overhead kick – a great way to get your first goal for the club – and later with a header. The next week we won 1–0 over Rangers with Hans again scoring, this time with a shot into the top corner from outside the box. For the rest of the season I held a regular place and saw my confidence grow.

The Scottish Cup was to provide the real drama that season. Away to Partick Thistle at a muddy Firhill was not the most glamorous of starts but we won 6–2. It was a good result, especially seeing as we conceded an early penalty. Willem Van der Ark scored a hat-trick that day. I wonder if he is the only foreign player ever to score a hat-trick in the Scottish Cup? Perhaps some statistically minded reader can prove me wrong!

In the next round we were at home to Morton. Just to make life interesting we again went behind before pulling through 2–1. I have to confess that for a while it looked like one of those days which make cup football so interesting, with a real possibility of high-flying Aberdeen going out to a club from a lower division. It was a typical cup-tie, being a hard battle on a muddy pitch, but we made it with goals from Hans Gillhaus and Charlie Nicholas.

In the quarter-final it was Hearts at home and we won 4–1. In the build-up to the game Hearts were sounding very confident, and their young striker Scott Crabb was saying what he was going to do to us. However all that just made Alex McLeish and me more determined than ever to be on our game. When we were 2–1 up and the game was in the balance a corner was half-cleared and I drove it home with my left foot. It was never going to be goal of the season but it helped us to progress in the cup.

In the semi-final we met Dundee United at Tynecastle in an east coast derby. There was a great atmosphere. At that stage both clubs were in the ascendancy as the 'new firm', seeking to compete with Rangers and Celtic. In the end we won comfortably, 4–0. I was fortunate to be in the right position to get the first goal. Brian Grant's header from Charlie Nicholas's cut-back was blocked by goalkeeper Alan Main and I was able to slot home the rebound.

I was initially credited with a second goal but I had to admit that while I would have liked to have claimed it, in fact it was Mixu Paatelainen who had put it into his own goal. One newspaper called it all a Mixu-p! Another paper's headline was 'Irvine owns up to prove honesty is the best policy.' I was also given the Tennents man-of-the-match award in that game.

Our last league game was a live TV game at Parkhead on 2 May. We needed to beat Celtic to make sure of finishing second in the league. With a young side we pulled it off 3–1, resting four or five of our senior players. So we approached the Scottish Cup final full of confidence. From my point of view things couldn't have been better. I was holding my place in the team, I had played in all the cup-ties leading up to the final and had even contributed two goals to the campaign.

During the ten days leading up to the cup final, the papers were full of speculation about whether Willie Miller would be recalled for the final in my place. The decision was between me, playing the biggest game of my career, or Willie Miller, with 853 games and several cup finals behind him. According to the papers I was having a 'severe dose of the Willies' all week, worried that Willie Miller would oust me from the team. In fact I knew I was playing.

On the way home from the Celtic league game, Alex Smith called me down to the front of the bus for a word. He said, 'There will be a lot in the press in the next week about Willie. Ignore it all. You are going to play. Don't let any of the press talk distract you. I am telling you now that you will be playing.' That was brilliant news for me, and it was so good for my confidence. Alex told me to keep it to myself, so in fact none of the other players knew that I had been told.

Aberdeen's approach to cup finals is very low-key. Some teams go away to a hotel for several days but we train as normal and just go down to Glasgow on the Friday night, as if it were a normal away game. There is no big build-up.

I was determined to enjoy the preparations and the experience of playing in the cup final. Unfortunately I picked up a knock so I was sweating a bit but I think it would have taken a broken leg to have stopped me from playing!

The game itself was a disappointment, 0–0 at full-time and 0–0 after extra time. To be honest there was precious little goal-mouth action. It seemed destined for penalties from before the end of normal time.

The final whistle went and the five Aberdeen penalty takers were named. I wasn't one of them, nor was I close to being chosen. It was a very nerve-racking situation but I was thinking, 'My involvement is over. I just have to watch the penalty shoot-out and hope that our boys can do their stuff.'

Celtic's Polish international Wdowczyk took the first penalty and put it wide, then Jim Bett scored to put us ahead. Peter Grant scored for Celtic, followed by Bobby Connor for Aberdeen. Paul McStay scored, then Hans Gillhaus made it 3–2. Tommy Coyne levelled it at 3–3, and then Brian Grant shot over the bar. Mike Galloway scored to put Celtic ahead for the first time at 3–4.

Charlie Nicholas was next and he scored. It was 4–4. He had

already agreed to leave Aberdeen and join Celtic at the end of the season. Now here he was with his last kick for Aberdeen Football Club trying to stop his new club from winning the cup and getting into Europe! He showed what being a professional footballer is all about by getting all that out of his mind and scoring the penalty.

As it moved into 'sudden death' with Celtic shooting first, the pressure was really on the Aberdeen players. As Celtic kept scoring, the Aberdeen players knew that if anyone missed Celtic had won the cup.

First to go in sudden death was Joe Miller, who had just been chosen as man of the match. He didn't blot his copybook. 5–4 to Celtic. We countered by nominating the Scottish Footballer of the Year, Alex McLeish. Goal, 5–5.

Derek Whyte scored for Celtic, 6–5.

Stewart McKimmie scored for Aberdeen, 6–6.

Paul Elliott scored for Celtic, 7–6.

Davie Robertson scored for Aberdeen, 7–7.

Dziekanowski scored for Celtic, 8–7.

Who would take the next penalty for Aberdeen? It was a measure of my self-confidence as a penalty-taker that I was more than happy to let 17 year-old Graeme Watson take the ninth penalty. He scored, 8–8.

Anton Rogan hit a good penalty which headed towards the bottom left corner. Theo Snelders took off, got his fingertips to the ball and pushed it around the post. Still 8–8.

There was nowhere to hide – I was down for the next penalty. There were only two Aberdeen players who had not taken penalties: goalkeeper Theo Snelders and me.

I was really nervous as I stepped up to take the kick but I just said a prayer and put my faith in God. The moment the ball hit the net was fantastic. It's a feeling I will never fully be able to describe. If I took another penalty tomorrow, I would probably miss, for I am not a good penalty-taker

I wasn't very confident. I just decided to hit it to the goalkeeper's left, and as I stepped up, I saw Pat Bonner gamble and move early to his right, so for a split second I knew that if I hit it properly I would score. The penalty shoot-out was at the Aberdeen end, so as the ball went in all the Aberdeen supporters erupted in a sea of red. Scoring the winning penalty was another landmark for me. So much of the time up to this point I had felt that I was learning my trade. Now I had been able to achieve something for the club.

Afterwards I was disappointed to be misquoted in the papers. The *Daily Record* had a headline 'God Won the Cup for Me'. What I said was that as I stepped forward to take the penalty the one thought in my mind was a fax I had received that day from Bruce Smith, one of the leaders of my church, saying 'remember you'll never walk alone'. As I walked forward to take the penalty I knew that I wasn't alone for God was with me.

After the cup final we went to the Craw's Nest in Anstruther and stayed overnight there with our wives joining us. It is a tradition with Aberdeen that the wives travel to the cup final together and then come and join the team on the Saturday night for a dinner and some kind of party.

On the Sunday morning Donna and I had breakfast with Bobby Mimms and his wife. Bobby had been on loan to Aberdeen earlier in the season and the club had invited him and his wife to the final. After breakfast we had a stroll down by the sea and I remember thinking that it seemed a million miles away from all that had gone on the last 24 hours. It was a lovely moment of peace and quiet in the midst of all the excitement.

Later in the day we went back to Aberdeen and drove through the city in an open-topped bus with possibly 30,000 people lining the route. We finished at the Town House where we went out on the balcony and showed off the cup.

There is no better way to finish a season. Playing in the cup final, winning the match and bringing home the cup is the pinnacle of anyone's season. The supporters really enjoy it but it is also a really special moment in any player's career.

6

PLAYING FOR SCOTLAND

Playing for Scotland has been the highlight of my career, but more than that, it has also been the fulfilment of a boyhood dream. When I was a boy, playing football with friends or even kicking a ball around on my own, in my imagination I was always playing for Aberdeen or for Scotland.

My dreams were realised and I got to play for Aberdeen and I love it. But that is my job, my bread and butter. Playing for Scotland is the ultimate. It is the wildest dream come true. Perhaps if you've played over 50 times for Scotland, like Alex McLeish and Willie Miller have, you get used to it, but I'm a long way from ever feeling that way.

From the moment I meet up with the Scotland squad for an international on the Saturday or the Sunday until I come home after the game on the Wednesday night or Thursday morning, the whole experience is just as exciting as it was in my boyhood dreams.

Playing for Scotland may have always been my dream but to be honest it was hardly a realistic ambition before 1990. When I was at Falkirk I played for Scotland at a semi-professional level but that is a far cry from the European Championships. I had never been capped by Scotland at Under-21 or B levels, and I had never been included in a squad until it all happened out of the blue when Scotland met Romania in 1990 in a qualifying match for the European Championship.

When the squad was named for the Romania game I just took my usual passing interest in it, to see which of my team-mates were included. Then one after another the central defenders dropped out. First Richard Gough, then Dave McPherson and Craig Levein pulled out. By the Saturday night it did occur to me that there were not many central defenders left to choose from and that I would never have a better chance.

I went to church as usual the next morning. One or two friends fuelled my excitement by asking if there was any word. They had been studying teletext and like me were wondering who else there was to pick. Just as I arrived home the phone was ringing. It was Alex Smith, the Aberdeen manager, asking where I had been all morning – he should have known I'd have been at church! He said that Andy Roxburgh had been in touch and wanted me to join the Scotland squad at Hampden Park at 4 p.m. that afternoon.

The excitement turned into a mad scramble as I packed a bag. Players' boots are kept at the club so I had to arrange to meet the club secretary, Ian Taggart, at Pittodrie to let me in to collect my boots and then it was off to Glasgow.

As I approached Glasgow I realised I had no idea how to find Hampden. I'd played at Hampden but had always gone on the team bus. I drove across Glasgow stopping every few minutes before eventually making it. The papers had fun next day writing about the new cap who is so green that he got lost on the way to Hampden!

For established players, internationals are a chance to meet up with old friends. Players love to exchange stories. Wages – especially what the English Premier League players are getting – is always a favourite topic of conversation. I was pleased just to be part of it.

The conversations about wages are interesting but not always helpful. If you discover that other players of a similar standard at another club are doing better financially, there is the temptation to think more about money than you should and to become dissatisfied. You can easily get yourself out of focus.

I met up with the squad at Hampden where we trained. Training is always very light on the Sunday as everyone has played for their clubs the previous day. We usually warm up, have a five-a-side match and practise ball skills for perhaps an hour.

After training we travel by bus to the hotel, the Marine Highland in Troon. I was sharing a room with Alex McLeish for the Romania game which made it all seem a bit more normal for me, especially as

56

he is not just a team-mate but also a good friend. That is very important as you spend a lot of time in your room. The key thing to remember in preparing for an international is to rest. On Sunday we have dinner together and then go back up to our rooms. On the Monday morning we train for an hour at Rugby Park, Kilmarnock, where the emphasis is on quality not quantity. Everything is short and sharp.

What really struck me on that first occasion was the standard. You have all the best players in Scotland together and the speed of thought and action is amazing. After lunch the afternoon was free for more rest. I was also impressed with the level of Andy Roxburgh's preparation. When I arrived I knew nothing about Romanian football, but by the time of the kick-off I knew the name of the person I would be marking and had seen enough video clips of him to have some idea of what to expect. Some of the players sometimes moan about having to go to the meetings to watch videos or talk about tactics. It was all new to me so I was delighted to be there.

On the Monday night the team watch one of the latest videos, and Tuesday follows the same pattern as Monday of training and rest. On Wednesday training is just really practising ball skills and going through the set pieces.

Normally the team is announced on Tuesday evening or Wednesday morning but on this occasion I was pretty sure from the start that I would play. What was in my favour was that they were looking for a player to play between Alex McLeish and Stewart McKimmie. Andy Roxburgh thought that picking me to play in a mini Aberdeen back four was his best option. Needless to say I was delighted to play with players I knew so well.

We go through the set pieces on the training ground so that if you are in the wall you know your place and with an attacking free-kick you know where you are making your run and so on. I found that much better than doing it on the blackboard.

The build-up to the game involves lunch, rest, then a snack, such as tea and toast and then the team-talk. I've always found Andy and Craig's team-talks inspiring. They stress the honour of representing your country, reminding you that it isn't just another match. I am always really fired up as I get on the bus to travel to the game.

The crowd for my first international was only 12,081 as the game was being screened on live television. Chants of 'if you hate the telly clap your hands' echoed round the ground. In a way, though, it was a help to me as an international debut in a packed Hampden could have been quite daunting.

With the birth of our first baby imminent, Donna travelled with a friend to the game – under strict instructions from her doctor not to get too excited! Donna was probably the calmest person around. So much so, in fact, that I remarked to her during the week after the game, 'If it had been me, I would have had the baby long ago with all the excitement.'

The game itself was an unforgettable experience, but the build-up was the one thing that I found hard to handle. Arriving at Hampden early, the players had a look at the pitch, a long warm-up, TV interviews – it all dragged on. Then when the time came for the players to go on to the pitch, there were still the national anthems to be played. While standing there in my Scottish international shirt was one of the proudest moments of my life, I just wanted to get on with the game.

The Scotland team that lined up against Romania on 12 September 1990 was Goram, McKimmie, Malpas, McAllister (sub Nevin), McLeish, Irvine, Robertson, McStay, McCoist, Macleod, Connor (sub Boyd).

In the early stages of the game the Romanians, displaying great skill, threatened to overrun Scotland. Romania took the lead in the 19th minute, John Robertson equalised after 37 minutes and then Ally McCoist scored after 75 minutes to set up a 2–1 win for Scotland. The *Daily Record* summed up the performance: 'Scotland have fielded better teams but none in recent times who tried so hard.' It was an exciting match to play in and even better was the fact that we won to get Scotland's European Championship campaign off to a good start.

The papers were generally satisfied with my performance. The *Record*'s assessment was: 'Nervous at the start but settled to give a promising show on his debut. Covered intelligently throughout.' The *Sun* reported: 'New boy Irvine slotted in like a veteran.'

I was retained in the squad for the next international, against Switzerland in October, but with everyone fit I didn't play. The next game was away against Bulgaria. Before the squad was named Andy Roxburgh rang me to say that he was leaving me out as there seemed no point in taking me to Sofia with no real prospect of playing. In the event the squad was hit by injuries and Andy did contact Aberdeen about adding me to the party, but in the meantime I too had picked up an injury.

It looked for a while as if I was going to be a one-cap-wonder. In fact it was two and a half years before I played for Scotland again. My second cap was against the world champions Germany in a friendly at Ibrox. The Scotland team that lined up for that game on 24 March 1993 was Walker, Wright, Boyd, Levein, Irvine, McLaren, Bowman, Ferguson, Collins, McInally, Robertson, with Scott Booth coming on as sub. The German team was: Kopke, Zorc, Helmer, Kohler, Thon, Buchwald, Klinsmann, Hassler, Riedle, Matthaus, Doll.

It was an exciting game with a great atmosphere provided by a 36,400 crowd at Ibrox –totally different from the small crowd for my first cap. We should have got something out of the game and it was frustrating that a defensive error gave them the goal. I was up against Jurgen Klinsmann and Karl-Heinz Riedle which certainly kept me on my toes. However, I also had three scoring chances – two headers and a shot – but didn't manage to find the net.

I appreciated some of the things the papers said the next day:

'Aberdeen centre-half Brian Irvine celebrated his second cap with a solid performance against world champions Germany.' *Press and Journal*

'Strong in the air . . . rarely drawn out of position.' *Daily Record*

'Irvine was the national embodiment of his national team's character against Germany: solid, honest, dependable and while without the wildest hint of being a world-beater, self-believing to the end.' *Scotland on Sunday*

I was also immensely grateful to Andy Roxburgh for his comments to the press after the game:

'Look at Brian Irvine. It has been two and a half years since he last played for us. He knows he's not an automatic choice and he goes out and plays his heart out. He just typifies the squad. He is simply someone we can trust. I thought Brian had an excellent game in defence and attack. Brian caused the Germans problems when he pushed forward for free-kicks and corners. He is the classic example of the good squad player any team needs to complement its more prominent players.

'Just as he did against Romania Brian proved he is reliable at international level. He is strong in the tackle and in the air. Despite his gentle media image he can be as hard as anyone in the game. Despite the fact that he stayed on the fringes of the squad after the Romania game, his attitude has been magnificent.' (*Green Final*, 27 March 1993)

Even before the game Andy had given me a real boost. He pointed out to me that a second cap was very significant. He said that lots of players get one cap but my getting a second one meant I had elevated myself above all the 'one-cap-wonders'.

Jürgen Klinsmann was also quoted in the *Green Final*:

'We knew the Scots had nothing to lose and would give more than 100 per cent to make up for their lack of experience. Their defenders stuck to their task and I don't think I have ever got so little room to work in an international.

'It also surprised me to learn it's been so long since Irvine gained his last cap. He is a big strong man and Scotland must be very lucky if they have enough good players to leave him out.'

In April 1993 Scotland lost 5–0 to Portugal in Lisbon. I was in the squad but not involved in the game. I watched the game from the stand in the Stadium of Light. Towards the end of the match I remember going down in the lift and hearing a big cheer. I thought it was 6–0 but fortunately Cadete, who now plays for Celtic, had just missed an open goal and the result stayed at 5–0.

Not playing in Lisbon may have worked in my favour. Richard Gough and Dave McPherson, who were the central defenders in that game, had their reputations damaged. That led to another opportunity for me.

The following month I was included in the squad for the World Cup qualifier against Estonia in Tallin on 19 May 1993. The procedure for an away game is obviously a bit different. You meet in Glasgow, train on Sunday afternoon at Hampden, stay in a hotel in Glasgow on the Sunday night and fly out on the Monday morning. On the Monday night you train in the stadium under the lights and get your first look at it.

My memories of Tallin are of how run-down everything was. The stadium, the dressing-room and the facilities were much poorer than we are used to. I don't mean that as a criticism. It was just an eye-opener to see the poverty of the country.

The Scotland team which beat Estonia 3–0 was Gunn, Wright (sub McLaren), Boyd, McStay, Hendry, Irvine, Gallacher, Bowman, Robertson (sub Booth), McClair, Collins. It was nice to play in front of Bryan Gunn again, in a reunion of the Aberdeen reserve team from the '80s!

After the game Andy Roxburgh was very complimentary about me, speaking of me as a possible future Scotland captain.

The home game with Estonia came just three weeks later on 2 June 1993 and I was picked again. The team was Gunn, McLaren (sub McKimmie), Boyd, McStay, Hendry, Irvine, Gallacher, Ferguson (sub Booth), McClair, Collins, Nevin.

A particular thrill for me was that the game was at Pittodrie. There have only been three internationals at Pittodrie in recent years and I've played in two of them. Alex McLeish with his 77 caps has only played one international in Aberdeen yet two of my first five were at Pittodrie, so I feel really lucky. It did seem strange, though, to come to a game at Pittodrie in the coach, instead of driving as I usually do.

We won 3–1 against Estonia. In the second half, I came up for a corner and tried an overhead kick but didn't get hold of it. Bearing in mind the fact that I was playing for Scotland and at Pittodrie, if that had gone in I think I would have retired on the spot, recognising that I could only go downhill from there!

The World Cup qualifier against Switzerland at Pittodrie on 8 September 1993 was really special. There was a full house, and the atmosphere was incredible. There were 3,000 visiting fans, making up a sea of red. At the warm-up the pipe band at one point played 'Amazing Grace'. This was an inspiration going into the match, and was also very moving as I listened to the tune and thought of the words whilst warming up.

Our team was: Gunn, McKimmie, Robertson, Bowman (sub O'Donnell), Irvine, McAllister, Levein, Collins, Booth (sub Jess), Durie, Nevin. It was Andy Roxburgh's last game as Scotland manager and we were determined to give him a great send off, but in the end had to settle for a 1–1 draw.

The next month all roads led to Rome when I lined up on 13 October 1993 in the Olympic Stadium against Italy in a World Cup qualifier. The team was Gunn, McKimmie, McLaren, Irvine, Boyd, Bowman (sub McStay), Jess (sub Durrant), McAllister, Gallacher, Durie, McCall. The Italian team, a real 'who's who' of football, was: Pagliuca, Mussi, Baresi, Costacurta, Benarrivo, Eranio, D. Baggio, Donadoni, R. Baggio, Stroppa, Casiraghi.

The Olympic Stadium was the best I've ever played in, and there was a good crowd of 61,178. We got off to a terrible start, losing two goals in the first 16 minutes to Donadoni and Casiraghi. I was beginning to think that while it was great to be here in Rome playing for Scotland, if we were going to lose 6–0 I wasn't too keen to be a part of it.

The first goal went under Bryan Gunn, and I know he was disappointed not to save it. The second goal just illustrated the level at which we were playing. Baggio had the ball, and he came inside to the edge of the box. I was marking Casiraghi. In a Premier League game, when a player makes a run it is usually after the ball is played and if you are quick enough you will get the tackle in. This time Casiraghi had gone before the ball so no matter how quick I was he had already gone and had got his shot in past Bryan Gunn.

Kevin Gallacher got one back almost immediately and at half-time we were only 2–1 down and feeling more comfortable. One incident with Baggio that disappointed me was when he left his foot up in a challenge with Bryan Gunn. It probably looked accidental to most people but I had a good view and saw that he didn't need to do it.

We stayed in the game for most of the second half. I had one header from a corner which went just wide. If only . . . A great strike by Eranio in the 81st minute then made the game safe for Italy.

The Italians were incredible. Their movement off the ball is almost telepathic. In the domestic game the ball is played through and then players react, but the Italians are able to anticipate the pass and there is no one more adept at it than Baggio. He also has a tough side to his game which makes him a more difficult opponent.

One thing which made the game in Rome special was that my friend Doug turned up. He had some business to do in Rome and managed to time it to fit in with the game. On the Tuesday evening, instead of watching a film with the team, I was able to slip away and spend some time with Douglas and his companion Jim Wilson, also from the church. We were also able to pray together.

I was again in the Scotland team which beat Malta 2–0 on 17 November 1993, in a World Cup qualifier at Ta Quali. The team was Leighton, McLaren, Hendry, McKinnon, Irvine, Durrant (sub Boyd), McAllister, McKinlay (sub Booth), Nevin, Ferguson, Gallacher.

I played too against Austria when we opened the new Ernst Happel Stadium in Vienna on 20 April 1994. We went behind to a spectacular volley from Hutter but we came back to win 2–1 with goals from John McGinlay and Billy McKinlay. Our team was Leighton, McKimmie, McLaren, Hendry, Irvine, Boyd (sub Ferguson), McKinlay, McAllister, Collins (sub McCall), McGinlay (sub Shearer), Jess (sub Nevin).

At the end of the 1993–94 season I went to Canada with Aberdeen. We trained on astroturf at the Hamilton Cats American Football pitch and Roy Aitken caught me on the achilles. That was on the Monday, and I flew back on the following day to meet up with the Scotland team on the Wednesday. Flying overnight, losing sleep and carrying an injury was not the ideal preparation for the match. We flew to Holland on the Thursday morning for the game in Utrecht on Friday night, 27 May.

It was a difficult game for us. It was the last game of the season for all the players with nothing really at stake, whereas for the Dutch it was their last friendly before heading for the USA and the World Cup.

I wasn't 100 per cent but I played, helped by a painkiller. To be honest I didn't have much option as we didn't have any cover. In the end Holland won comfortably, 3–1, and they also missed a penalty. I got on the scoresheet but not as I would have wanted. I went to cut out a cross and could only deflect the ball into my own net.

It was a real party atmosphere with one fan in particular, with a trombone, making his presence felt. I was up against Ruud Gullit, in what was his last game for Holland. Most people say that Gullit had a row with the manager and decided not to play for Holland any more but I like to think it was because I marked him so tightly that he decided to give up! In fact he didn't even come out for the second half.

The Dutch team that night was De Goey, Valckx, Jonk, Frank de Boer, Winter, Wouters, Witschge, Ronald de Boer (sub Numan), Overmars, Gullit (sub Van Vossen), Roy (sub Taument). We lined up with Leighton (sub Gunn), Clarke, Hendry, Irvine, McKimmie, McCall, McKinlay (sub Nevin), McAllister, Collins (sub Ian Ferguson), McGinlay (sub Shearer), Durie (sub Jess).

I know we lost the three games against Holland, Germany and Italy but, as a player, you can't ask for any more than to play against teams like that and in such fantastic stadia. It gave us the opportunity to be tested against the best teams and players in the world.

Holland was my last appearance for Scotland – so far – although I was in the squad for the next game against Finland, in the Euro 96 qualifying competition. An interesting point is that I played in the first game in the European Championship campaign which led to Scotland qualifying for Sweden in 1992, and was also in the squad for the first game in the successful qualification for Euro 96. So if Scotland want to make it to the European Championships in the year 2000, they know who to pick for the first qualifying game!

Question: how many Scotland caps do I have? The answer is either nine or six. The rules on caps have changed since I got my first one. It used to be one cap per season but now you get a cap for any competitive game and also one cap per season if you play in friendlies but not competitive matches that season. So while I have played nine times for Scotland I have only got six actual caps.

I have also got a nice collection of shirts. When you play for Scotland you get two sets of the full kit, which allows you to swap one with a player in the opposition and still have one to keep. If I get one more cap I'll be able to kit out a whole outfield team!

I swapped with Karl-Heinz Riedle in the German game and Casiraghi in the Italian game. It was an emotional moment at the end of the Italian game when Casiraghi embraced me and we swapped jerseys. In the Holland game the swapping took place after the game in the dressing-room. A Dutch official came in and asked for the Scottish shirts which were to be swapped. Three of the boys offered their shirts, including me, but when the official came back he had only two Dutch shirts and I didn't get one. I went into the Dutch dressing-room to see what was happening and all the players had gone. There was just one official there. Then Willie Miller (who was helping the Scottish manager for that game) stepped in and gave me a Dutch number 10 shirt that he had been given at the end of the match.

There is a small match fee for international games, but unless you qualify for the World Cup or European Championships where there might be a particular bonus scheme or sponsorship deal, you won't get rich playing for Scotland. To be honest, I would pay to play for Scotland if I had to!

It's amazing that in my nine appearances for Scotland I have played against some of the biggest teams in Europe – World Champions Germany, and Holland and Italy as well. The Olympic Stadium in Rome is as big a stage as there is in world football. At times I have had to ask myself 'Is it really me out there on the same pitch as Gullit, Klinsmann or Baggio?' It seemed unreal. It would have been easy to have been overawed, but I just told myself that we were all human, and I did my best.

I feel privileged to have been allowed to play in such exalted company and to fulfil my dreams by playing for Scotland.

7

AN EPIC STRUGGLE FOR THE CHAMPIONSHIP

The 1990–91 season was another good one for Aberdeen and for me personally. We were again in Europe as cup winners, and we were in contention for the league championship until the last game of the season.

Pre-season again took us to Holland where I played in matches against Veloc Eindhoven and Twente Enschede where we recorded a win and a draw. Three games against Scottish league sides completed our preparations for the season.

The previous season had ended with elation for me in the Scottish Cup final drama but in bitter disappointment for Willie Miller, who was not selected for the final. Willie was determined not to let his injury beat him, and he started pre-season but was obviously struggling. He played in a game against Queens Park at Hampden in the Skol Cup, which was our first competitive game of the season.

It was funny to start the new season at Hampden, where we had finished the previous one. The game could have turned into a nightmare for us when Queens Park took the lead late in the game, but fortunately we were able to come back and win it 2–1. That game, however, was to prove to be Willie Miller's last game for Aberdeen.

I had, over the course of the previous season, established myself in the team alongside Alex McLeish. With Willie Miller retiring as a player and coaching the reserves, I just carried on in that position. The season started well for me and then in September I got my international call-up for the Romania game. That was a really exciting time for me with one important game following another. A Skol Cup quarter-final for Aberdeen was followed by a European Nations qualifying match at Hampden and a European Cup Winners' Cup tie for Aberdeen in Cyprus. I felt that I could not ask for any more in terms of the level of football I was experiencing.

What a difference a year makes! During that month I was using the same Bible study guide that I had used the previous year. It was interesting to compare some of the comments written the previous year with my present feelings. In 1989 I had written, 'Feeling very low about football' at a time when I was out of the team. A year later I had a Scottish Cup winner's medal, a Skol Cup winner's medal, a Scottish cap – not to mention a baby!

The one thing on my mind on the trip to Cyprus for the Cup Winners' Cup tie was that Donna was at home expecting our first baby. As a result there were a few long phone calls on my bill from the hotel in Cyprus on that trip! Fortunately Hannah delayed her birth until after I got back.

She was born on 25 September. The birth of your first child is an incredibly moving experience. Donna was very quick with the birth; we got to the hospital at 7 o'clock and Hannah was born at 10.20. For me it was an incredible high, to witness the birth of a child and to realise all that it means. It was period of great domestic happiness which was reflected in my football as well.

We had a good run in the Skol Cup, beating Stranraer 4–0 with me among the scorers, and Hearts 3–0. However, we lost 1–0 to Rangers in the semi-final of the Skol Cup. It was funny, though – for the first time in my life losing didn't really matter, so happy was I about being a father.

I had met up with the team the day after Hannah's birth. I was floating. On the night, though, we just didn't play well. Trevor Steven got a lucky break and made the most of it with a goal. One of our defenders was trying to clear the ball but Trevor charged it down, it fell right into his path and he went through and scored. We didn't really create any chances and rather let ourselves down.

Some of the boys felt that the build-up had been too low-key and that it had not felt as if we were playing a in semi-final. We had not been sufficiently motivated, and Hans Gillhaus disappointed us all by going to Holland to play in a friendly (he was chosen as substitute) instead of playing for us in an important semi-final. This put a big question mark over his commitment to Aberdeen, and by the time Willie Miller took over in early 1992 he wasn't figuring in the team and didn't do so for the rest of the season.

Whatever the reason was, we were out of the cup.

We lost 5–0 to St Johnstone the following Saturday, the heaviest defeat I have ever experienced playing for Aberdeen, although unfortunately matched by our 5–0 defeat by Celtic in the 1995–96 season. The St Johnstone defeat really hurt and brought me back down to earth with a jolt. Before the match we lost Alex through injury; Davie Robertson was sent off; Bobby Connor, who had just moved house the day before the game, gave away a penalty. We were 3–0 down at half-time. It was a real humiliation and we are never allowed to forget it, as St Johnstone always delight in mentioning it in their programme when we play at McDiarmid Park.

We bounced back to win 3–0 over Famagusta and progressed to the next round of the Cup Winners' Cup for a tie with Legia Warsaw. Then we played Rangers at Pittodrie in some of the worst conditions I have ever played in. There had been a rainstorm all morning and without wishing to criticise the referee, Les Mottram, I did not think that the game should have been played.

After about an hour, Theo Snelders came to cut out a cross and Ally McCoist went for the ball, flying through the air, and caught Theo on the cheek. He suffered a depressed cheekbone and was stretchered off. I went in goal and managed to keep a clean sheet as we drew 0–0. In that game I felt a pain in my abdomen. It was the first sign of an injury which was to require surgery at the end of the season.

Theo was out for two months, replaced initially by Andy Dibble and then by Mike Watt, who is of course now our first-choice keeper. Incidentally, Mike is nicknamed 'Skittle' by Duncan Shearer, because he seems to let in a lot of goals in training, saving as many as a skittle would in the middle of the goal! Seriously, though, Mike has now established himself as the number one goalkeeper after a long time as understudy to Theo and is growing in stature and confidence.

The next big game was against Legia Warsaw. The first leg was at Pittodrie, where we expected them to sit back in typical European away leg fashion. In fact they came at us and hit the bar early on. We had our chances but had to settle for a 0–0 draw, which isn't such a bad result in Europe – at least we had not let them score an away goal.

A few months prior to the game someone had given me a copy of the book *Goal Behind the Curtain* by Cliff Rennie (Christian Focus Publications 1990). The book tells the fictional story of a Christian footballer, Doug Mackay, who plays for the Scottish Premier League club, Dalkirk. In the UEFA Cup the team was drawn successively against teams from Czechoslovakia, Romania and Albania. Each time Doug is asked to take Bibles to Christians in the country where he is to play. With a few adventures, he succeeds.

An irony in the book is that one of the European ties is settled by the penalty shoot-out. Doug, who hates taking penalties, is the ninth player called upon, and he scores the winning penalty. Now where else have we heard about a reluctant penalty-taker, scoring the winner late on in the penalty shoot-out?

Not only had I read the book, but when I went to speak at a church, I met the author, Cliff Rennie. So when I flew to Warsaw with the Aberdeen squad, I was carrying not only a few Bibles in Polish and Russian but also a gift from our church to a church in Warsaw. The flight was delayed, which made me a little apprehensive about this meeting with the Polish Christian who was to collect the Bibles and the gift from Deeside Church. But no sooner had I entered the hotel than a stranger walked up to me and asked, 'Are you Brian Irvine?' I was delighted to hand over the gifts and to thank God for working everything out. The sum that I handed over was substantial but it was made even bigger by my taking it in dollars which were particularly valued in Poland. I was told that $10 was the average monthly wage for a working man in Poland at that time.

In the away leg, we conceded a goal with six minutes to go. Looking back, we had again gone close in Europe but not quite managed to pull it off. Legia went on to the semi-final before losing to Manchester United, the eventual winners, and we were left to think about what might have been. As I left the field I was spat on and jeered by some Polish fans. However, in view of the gift and the Bibles that I had been able to bring, there had at least been an element of victory in the bitter defeat.

Our league form continued to be good and we were in second place for most of the season. I got two league goals against Dunfermline and St Mirren – why do I always score against St Mirren? I played in 29 of the 36 league games that season and, ironically, three of the games that I missed were in the run-in. I was not picked for the games against St Johnstone and Motherwell, nor for the league decider against Rangers.

Part of the reason I was left out was that I was struggling with my fitness. The pain in my abdomen was such that I was only getting through the games with the aid of painkillers, which obviously wasn't ideal, but which had really been the case since the Rangers game in October. At this time I found myself with a new name. For a while I was having an injection before every game, and the papers picked this up and wrote about how brave I was. Some of the lads started to call me John Wayne or Wayno.

If our league form was good we made a disappointing job of defending the cup, losing 1–0 at Pittodrie to Motherwell. Whether because I was struggling or simply because they felt it was the best option at the time, the managers decided to play Stewart McKimmie alongside Alex in the centre of the defence. After the team was named for the league decider against Rangers, Jocky Scott turned to me and said, 'Brian, I'm sorry. There's nothing I can say.' I appreciated that and I replied, 'It doesn't matter about me. The important thing is that we win the league today.'

It was a disappointment but I respected Jocky and Alex and felt they had handled it as well as possible. I think too that they appreciated my attitude. The nice thing is that we have remained friends after they moved on. Alex is now manager of Clyde while Jocky is at Hibs.

The league championship had built up to a great finale. We had to play the last game at Ibrox with the championship in the balance. Going into the game we were on a run of 12 games without defeat – 11 wins and a draw. What's more, Rangers had lost 3–0 to Motherwell the previous week.

We went into the game equal on points with Rangers and equal on goal difference. However, we were ahead of Rangers in the league table by virtue of having scored more goals. A draw would therefore be enough to give us the title.

It was our fifth meeting with Rangers that season. In the league, it had been two draws and a win for Aberdeen but Rangers had beaten us in the Skol Cup. We changed from the 4–3–3 formation which had been successful for us all season to 4–4–2 and brought in Peter van de Ven to get the point we needed. It looked like a negative approach.

I think the opposite is true. If Alex and Jocky had taken the easy option and left it at 4–3–3, nobody would have blamed them, but they took the gamble and changed the system to 4–4–2. They emphasised at the team-talk that this was not defensive, and in fact in the first ten minutes we created two great chances for Hans Gillhaus and Peter van de Ven, but neither went in.

Some people say that Alex and Jocky fell out about the team for the match. Personally I doubt that, but it certainly seemed that they never really recovered from the defeat.

I remember feeling devastated afterwards that we had come so close to winning the championship only to be pipped at the post. In a way I was shielded a bit from it by not being in the team, but I still felt it just as much. The fear is that I might never get as good a chance to win the league as that day. We had started the season 36 games away from winning the league. We had come within one hour of doing it but we had still failed. You would still fancy Rangers to win with home advantage but they did have some injury problems for that match.

Towards the end of that season I had the opportunity to take part in a Scottish Television programme, *Dana's Day Out*, which was shown throughout the UK. I really enjoyed doing it especially as Donna and Hannah were able to come with me. It was also a nice break from the routine of training. I was interviewed about my Christian faith on the ship, *Sir Winston Churchill*, off the Ayrshire coast. I was slightly caught out when Dana said to me, 'As you are from Aberdeen I assume that you are an experienced sailor.' I had to admit that for all Aberdeen's associations with the sea, it was actually my first experience on the water. Dana was such a lovely lady. The next time we met was Christmas 1994 when she was playing Snow White in panto in the Capitol in Aberdeen. She seems to look younger the older she gets.

In 1991 I got closer to the FA Cup than the Scottish Cup. I was in hospital in London recovering from an operation for a condition called 'Gilmour's groin', named after the surgeon who first performed the operation. I had the operation a day or two before the FA Cup final between Nottingham Forest and Tottenham Hotspur and was able to watch the game on TV in the hospital. It was the cup final in which Paul Gascoigne was carried from the field injured and taken straight to hospital.

At the time I didn't give any thought to which hospital he would be taken to. However, that evening I discovered that he was on the floor below me, when the rest of the Tottenham team turned up to show him the cup.

Security was tight and I didn't get to see him but I left a note to encourage him which was delivered by one of the nurses. When I left the hospital I was surprised to see a real crowd of pressmen and photographers. It was nice of them to give me such a good send-off! Of course they were more interested in a picture of Gazza than of me. He really has had to live an unreal life whilst playing professional football in England, Italy and now in Scotland.

I had one more appearance to make at Pittodrie, which was a bit different from the other 20 that season. The American evangelist, Billy Graham, was conducting Mission Scotland. He was speaking first at Pittodrie and then at Parkhead, and I was asked to take part and say what it meant to me to be a Christian. It was particularly exciting for me to have the chance to share my faith with thousands on the pitch at Pittodrie, my place of work, and it was an incredible experience to be on the platform with Billy Graham himself.

The meeting at Parkhead was transmitted to churches all over Britain via a live satellite link. Whether for that reason or for some other, I was very nervous beforehand but also honoured and grateful to have been given the chance to do it. It was a joy to meet the members of the Billy Graham team. What really struck me about them was that for members of such a world-wide mission team, they were all so humble.

One important effect of my appearance at Mission Scotland was that I became more widely known nationally as a Christian. My profile as a Christian had been raised which resulted in my receiving more and more invitations to speak about my Christian faith, not just in the Aberdeen area but throughout Scotland. However, because of the publicity surrounding my involvement with the Billy Graham campaign, some people put two and two together and made five. I had one or two tabloid journalists at my front door and on the phone asking me if there was any truth in the rumour that I was giving up football to become a minister in the church. Perhaps it was because I was involved in such a high profile Christian event and had been missing from the team for the last few games of the season in the title run-in that people started the rumour. I will never know.

The truth was, of course, that I was out of the team partly because of the groin injury and the excellent form of Stewart and Alex. I had no intention whatsoever of retiring from professional football, but perhaps that did not make such a good story in the newspapers!

In 1989 there had been enquiries from a few clubs about whether I was available for transfer as I was not a regular first-team player. Charlton Athletic, Crystal Palace and Dundee made enquiries but were told that I was not for sale. The fact that teams were expressing an interest in me boosted my confidence, but I am glad now that I never had to make the choice about whether or not to leave Aberdeen.

8

WILLIE MILLER IN CHARGE

The 1991–92 season was always going to be a difficult one. We had come so close to winning the league the previous year. There was almost bound to be a hangover.

We had a good start to pre-season with some solid fitness work, then we went off to Bermuda on tour. It was a mammoth journey, flying via New York, where we stayed overnight. The problem was that it was the wrong place at the wrong time. New York and Bermuda were exciting places to go to and would have been ideal for an end of season tour. However, we were here for a week's serious work in preparation for the new season.

In New York we were staying in a hotel at the JFK airport, but with us being in a city that none of us had ever visited before, the lads all wanted to go and explore. However, we were about half an hour out of the city and already jet-lagged, and the management wanted us just to have an early night. Unfortunately the incident created some bad feeling and got the trip off to a bad start.

The management were right but the lads were upset to miss an opportunity to see an exciting city. Davie Winnie was caught by the boys writing on a postcard, 'Life is fast and furious in the Big Apple.' He got a bit of stick for it as life for us was anything but 'fast and furious'! He is still reminded about the postcard by the boys.

On the positive side we were being given the chance to see something of Bermuda, a really beautiful part of the world, but the training wasn't very good. Jocky seemed quite tense and we sensed that something wasn't quite right. The heat and the humidity every day during training didn't help either.

We played two games against the Bermudan national team. I played in the second one and was delighted to be playing again in what was my first game since the operation, especially as we won 4–0. Personally my memories of Bermuda are good – a successful comeback game in a beautiful place. There was even a church at the end of the road so I was able to go along there.

Whilst at church I met an exiled Scot, Michael Whalley, who was a long-distance runner in his spare time. We had a free day on the Sunday and he took me on a whistle-stop tour of this paradise island. If you ever have the time and the money I would recommend a visit to this little island with its colourful houses, blue seas, golden beaches, British customs and, from what we saw, friendly people. Our reservations were just that it wasn't the place for pre-season work.

My first game at Pittodrie that season was against Manchester United in a challenge match where I was up against Mark Hughes. He is a really tough competitor who is very skilful at holding up the ball and shielding it to allow his midfielders and other forwards to link up and attack us. It finished 1–1 and then Manchester United won a penalty shoot-out. After six months depending on painkillers it was just nice for me to be playing without needing them. Theo Ten Caat marked his home debut with a beautiful strike for our goal. It was great to see Alex Ferguson back at Pittodrie and for his son, Darren, to be in the team.

My first league game was back in my home town against Airdrie, who were newly promoted to the Premier League. The icing on the cake was that I scored our first competitive goal of the season. (I gave my home town a hard time that season, scoring again later in the season as we beat them 1–0.) We won that opening game 2–1 and followed it with two more wins to leave us with three wins out of three after the first week of the season.

Shortly afterwards, however, Airdrie came to Pittodrie and knocked us out of the Skol Cup, sowing the first seeds of doubt about our season. After the defeat our league form was a bit up and down. Then we lost 1–0 at home to Copenhagen in the UEFA Cup, which was the signal for the start of the supporters' murmurings for a change of management. Jocky Scott decided to leave to become manager of Dunfermline. That was a shock to the players as we had looked on Jocky and Alex as a pair. We were more shocked that the partnership was breaking up than we would have been if the two of them had left together. I felt that the two of them had worked well together and that neither of them would be as effective without the other. Alex continued on his own for the time being, however.

We had a good 2–0 win at Ibrox. Whatever the context, and whatever the competition, it is always good to beat Rangers. The only disappointment was that I got a yellow card.

I have never been sent off, a record which I would certainly want to preserve until I retire. Having said that, to get a red card today you only have to handle the ball in a reflex action or mistime a tackle when you are the last man. You could, of course, make the same tackle in another situation and only get a booking or not even that. I have been booked nearly 40 times. If I have gone into a tackle with the genuine aim of winning the ball and been clumsy or late, then I accept the booking. I can't recall ever going into a tackle deliberately intending to foul someone, although at times I have been a bit wound up by something that has just happened in the game and have been a bit over-eager. My bookings, though, are usually down to a lack of skill on my part resulting in a clumsy tackle, or indeed the skill or speed of the forward taking the ball away from where I was tackling.

In my early days at Falkirk and again when I moved up in standard to Aberdeen, two things contributed to a lot of bookings. One was over-enthusiasm, when I was just trying too hard to succeed, and the other was not quite adjusting to the pace of the game. Sometimes too an instruction from the manager to play it tight and put in some hard tackles can put you under pressure. On a few occasions I have committed what probably looked to the crowd like a bad foul. It may just be that the forward's skill and speed had taken the ball away when I was already committed to the tackle.

An interesting statistic is that two-thirds of my bookings have been in away games. When playing away from home as a defender the home crowd is baying for your blood. When a tackle goes in on a home forward, the crowd reaction is probably a contributory factor to the higher proportion of bookings received in away games. In making this observation I imply no criticism of referees.

One type of booking that I have never had and which I would hope never to get is for dissent. It is always wrong, although in the heat of the moment it is easy to understand why it happens.

I am a Christian in everyday life and hope that it is reflected in my football. Out on the park I want to do the right things and cheating is not one of them. I am conscious of the need to set an example to those who are watching.

I confess that there was one match where I was moaning a bit at the ref, but he soon put me in my place. I was about to take a free-kick when someone stopped in front of the ball to delay the kick. I turned to the ref to protest. He replied, 'Shut up, Brian. I've left one like you at home washing the dishes; I don't need you going on at me all afternoon!'

The win over Rangers was followed by our exit from the UEFA Cup. After losing the home leg we were always going to be up against it in the away leg. My own memory of the game, I am afraid, is of having the ball under no real pressure and turning to pass back to Theo Snelders without seeing that Jensen had stayed in the box. He was able to intercept the back pass and put us further behind. I was really disappointed and felt that I had let everyone down.

The following Saturday I scored against St Mirren. I was so determined to score that I was in the box at every opportunity. Somehow I was desperate to make up for the disappointment of Wednesday and to atone for my error. We won 4–1, interestingly with Roy Aitken in the St Mirren team. The win put us top of the table. However, we hit a bad spell with six defeats, a win and a draw in eight matches, which took us down to sixth place in the league.

One memorable match for me was against Hibernian at Easter Road. Keith Wright was through and I tried to tackle him and brought him down. I was probably a bit fortunate not to be sent off but perhaps there was another Aberdeen player in the box. As I was not the last defender, it fortunately did not result in an automatic red card.

Theo Snelders was so annoyed at the award of the penalty that he challenged Keith Wright and accused him of diving. They had an argument and Theo lifted his hand and was sent off. Theo kicked the ball over the Easter Road stand and it disappeared into the night sky, never to be seen again. At that time there was no substitute goalkeeper, so I went in goal. Pat McGinlay took the penalty, hard but straight. I stood up, blocked it and dived on it as he came in for the rebound.

So in the space of about two minutes, I had conceded a penalty, seen our keeper sent off, put on the goalkeeper's jersey and saved the penalty. We had a good chance to score ourselves when we also earned a penalty but Jim Bett shot over. Then, three minutes into injury time, Theo Ten Caat lost possession and let Hibs get a cross in and Danny Lennon stuck it past me. We had lost 1–0 after putting up such a fight and battling on with ten men.

We were without Alex McLeish for much of this period and I am sure that had a lot to do with our poor performances during this spell. We beat Hearts 4–0 with Scott Booth and Eoin Jess having excellent games and scoring three of the goals between them, despite being up against Scotland defenders Craig Levein and Davie McPherson.

Having gone out of the Skol Cup at the first hurdle and not really looking as if we were going to do much in the league, the Scottish Cup took on added importance. We played Rangers in the third round in a live TV game. We played pretty well but went down 1–0 to an Ally McCoist goal. Andy Goram had an outstanding game. I remember a save from me in the last minute from close in. After he saved it I fell to my knees, thinking, 'how did he ever get to that?' It was pure reflex.

With the exit from the cup the writing was more than ever on the wall for Alex Smith. A draw with Dunfermline was followed by a 1–0 defeat at home to Hibs who beat us with a goal in the last minute for the second time. That proved to be Alex Smith's last game as Aberdeen manager. I look back on the day with sadness as I recall Alex Smith calling us all together to tell us the news. There were players who had tears in their eyes when the meeting was over.

The directors felt it was time for a change. Willie Miller, who was at that time the youth team coach, was the popular choice, although inexperienced as a manager, having stopped playing only the season before.

As a result of the publicity I had received through appearing with Billy Graham, at that stage I was receiving a lot of invitations to speak at churches throughout Scotland. When I was doing a lot of speaking the regime was punishing, yet I believe God gave me the energy to do it. It was hard for Donna, though. I would leave home on Friday morning to train and travel to an away game, then perhaps stay over Saturday night in Glasgow to speak somewhere on the Saturday night or on the Sunday. I would get home on Sunday afternoon and be back at work on the Monday.

Usually after the meeting there was a crowd of people wanting to meet me and to get my autograph. This could easily have led to a conflict. On the one hand, I wanted to be polite to the people and give them my time. On the other hand, I wanted to get away because I was tired, had a three-hour journey home and had to be in training the next day.

As I shared my faith and spoke of its importance in my life, the response of people wanting my autograph was often such an anti-climax. I just hope and pray that from the many meetings I spoke at, an autograph of Brian Irvine is not the only thing people took away with them.

I always tried to be professional about the speaking and was careful not to arrange to speak the night before a game. On the few occasions when I had arranged to stay over after an away game for a speaking engagement and the manager decided to have an extra training session on the Sunday, he was usually quite flexible and understanding. If I said that I had a long-standing engagement I was excused from training.

I used to sit down at the beginning of the season with all the invitations to speak that I had received and the fixture list and work out which speaking engagements would fit in with which away games. With hindsight I now see that I was doing too much speaking, but the opportunities were there and I wanted to tell people about Jesus. I believe too that God kept me safe in my travelling and gave me the energy to do it. I did speaking on this scale for about three years; it was very much part of my schedule.

Willie Miller's first game in charge was against Rangers. We were in fact due to play Rangers on 20 February 1992, and on this occasion I had agreed to speak at Ayr Baptist Church. Someone was to pick me up at Ibrox, take me to Ayr for the meeting and get me on a train back home. We travelled down to Glasgow as usual on the Friday. However, torrential rain on the Saturday morning led to the game being called off before lunch-time. The team was heading back to Aberdeen and we were going to train in the afternoon. I explained to

Willie that I had agreed to speak in Ayr but I still had to go back with the team. We finished training at 4 p.m. and I set off for Ayr, Douglas Smith driving me in a four-wheel drive vehicle. The rain was horrendous and we did not reach Ayr until about 8.45 p.m. I gave the talk and we set off for Aberdeen, getting back at about 2 a.m. Quite an eventful day!

The Rangers game was rearranged for the Tuesday, so on the Monday I found myself setting off for Glasgow for the third time in four days. The team was keyed up with everyone keen to make an impression on the new manager. We did okay and came away with a 0–0 draw.

Our form was mixed to the end of the season. One game that stands out for me was a 1–0 win over my home-town team, Airdrie, when I was able to score the only goal. Again I was speaking in Glasgow after the game and drove to Lenzie and back on the Saturday, as the next day was Mothers Day and I wanted to be home with Donna and Hannah.

It was disappointing to finish sixth in the league that season, especially after being so narrowly beaten into second place the previous year. The simple fact was that we did not win enough games, with 14 draws and 13 defeats accompanying our 17 wins.

However, for me personally it had been a good year, as I picked up several awards including the Association of Aberdeen Supporters' Clubs' player-of-the-year award. This is a prestigious title awarded to the overall player of the year voted for by about 40 supporters' clubs.

During that season John Milne, who was also a Christian, was signed for Aberdeen. We used to meet together every Friday after training and sit, usually in the dug-out, and talk and pray together. Sometimes Derek Adams, a young player, joined us. Derek's father George was a good friend to me. He had been an Aberdeen player with a promising future but several knee operations had ended his career. George has always been a great source of advice on anything to do with football, and it is a great disappointment to me that he is now working for Celtic as a scout and coach rather than for Aberdeen. He was available and keen to work for Aberdeen a year or two back but Celtic got in first. George has a TV repair shop in Urquart Road just round the corner from Pittodrie and I often pop round for some good advice from this warm, generous man and special friend.

John, Derek and I never sought to draw any attention to ourselves but sometimes other players saw us and if they asked, I was happy to tell them what we were doing. John was a good friend to me but sadly he never made it at Aberdeen. Actually, I'm not that sad, as he was a central defender and if he had made it, it might have been at my expense! He is now in Bristol working as a teacher and playing semi-professional football.

9

RUNNERS-UP

At the start of the 1992–93 season my contract had one year to go. After having had a good season in 1991–92, I decided to go to Willie Miller and say that I had no desire to leave Aberdeen but was keen to sign a new contract without waiting for my existing one to run out. I was offered a two year extension which I was delighted to sign.

I feel that the 1992–93 and 1993–94 seasons were probably the peak of my career in terms of level of performance and consistency. At the start of the 1992–93 season I still had just one international cap. By the end of the next season I had collected a further eight caps. That year, Aberdeen achieved a treble of runners-up places.

After Holland and Bermuda, Willie Miller chose the Highlands for our pre-season tour! It may not have been as glamorous but it was more effective and we made a good start to the season. We did reasonably well in the league, finishing a comfortable second to Rangers. The difference between us was well illustrated in our home form. Rangers won 20 out of 22 home games, while we had seven draws and two defeats at Pittodrie. In our four league meetings with Rangers, they won the first three, our only victory coming when they were already champions.

In the Skol Cup we started with a 4–0 win over Arbroath, followed by a 1–0 defeat of Dunfermline after extra time. In the quarter-final we beat Falkirk 4–1 with Duncan Shearer getting a hat-trick and me scoring the other goal.

Willie decided to change things for the Skol Cup semi-final, however, putting Gary Smith and Alex McLeish together in the centre of the defence. I had lost the regular place that I had held throughout the previous season. The team beat Celtic 1–0 in the semi-final and Willie kept the same defence for the final.

For the second time I had to face the disappointment of missing out on a cup final. As a player this is something that you just have to accept with as positive an attitude as is possible, but it is not easy. It depends partly on the stage of your career at which it happens. In 1986 when I was in the squad for the Scottish Cup final I was delighted, for I had never been in a cup final squad before. In 1992, however, I was an international player who was established in the first team and had come to expect to play in cup finals. It was quite hard to handle being left out this time. As I played 39 of 44 league games that season, it was ironic that the Skol Cup final should have come at the only time I was out of favour. However, I firmly believe – in life and in football – that it is not so much what happens that matters but the way in which you handle it. If you dwell on your disappointments, they can destroy you. However, if you keep your head up, things can turn around very quickly.

Aberdeen lost 2–1 to Rangers in the Skol Cup final. Shortly afterwards, Alex got an injury and I was back in the team. I played against Airdrie and went on to hold my place for the rest of the season. After the game I met up with Donna and we went to a Cliff Richard concert at Glasgow, where we had the opportunity of meeting him backstage beforehand, much to Donna's delight. I also enjoyed meeting this wonderful example of a Christian in the public eye.

A win at Dundee with Lee Richardson's last-minute winner and a win over Motherwell was followed by a game at Partick, where we were 2–0 up when the snow caused the game to be abandoned. I spoke at a church in Partick and got a bit of teasing about how Partick had got off the hook and would take us when the game was rearranged. The game took place on the following Tuesday and we put seven goals past them! The following Saturday we beat Hearts 6–2 and I scored.

We were really flying. At this point we were mounting a serious challenge to Rangers, with a sequence of seven straight wins and 12 wins and three draws in 15 games from 7 October to 2 February.

Unfortunately the sequence ended with a 1–0 defeat by Rangers at Pittodrie. Mark Hateley, so often the scorer of vital goals against us, rose above Steve Wright to head home the winner. We had our chances but again Andy Goram repeatedly denied us.

The winning sequence had included our second 7–0 win of the season, this time over Airdrie. A lot of the credit for this purple patch goes to a new striker! Starting with the Hearts game I scored five league goals in eight games, one each against Hearts, St Johnstone, Dundee United, Motherwell and Airdrie.

The Scottish Cup was under way by this stage. We beat Hamilton 4–1 and I scored again. In the next round we had a TV match against Dundee United. We won 2–0 and Jock Brown commented that I was having my best season ever.

The years 1990–93 saw me at my peak. I remember thinking that it was a privilege to be playing so well and, to be picked as first choice for Scotland, being recognised as one of the two best centre-halfs in the country. I was constantly giving thanks to the Lord for giving me the ability to play at this level.

The quarter-final was against Clydebank and I think we were a bit complacent. If we could put seven past a Premier League team on more than one occasion, surely we only had to turn up to beat Clydebank from the First Division. We were 1–0 up and coasting. I hit the bar with a header, and then in the last minute Martin McIntosh got the equaliser with a spectacular free-kick. The game was marred by Eoin Jess breaking his leg. It was a real tragedy, as he was playing so well at the time.

The replay at Kilbowie Park was an entertaining game. It was a very wet night and a typical Scottish Cup tie. We got off to a good start and I scored one of my best goals ever, hitting a shot on the turn to put us one up. Mixu Paatelainen made it 2–0 and we seemed safe. However, Clydebank got a goal back just before half-time, and then scored twice more in the second half to go 3–2 ahead. But Theo Ten Caat had a great free-kick against the bar and Scott Booth followed up to score from the rebound. It was 3–3. Scott scored our winner when the game seemed to be heading for extra time.

We beat Hibs 1–0 in the semi-final at Tynecastle. It was a drab affair with Scott Booth scoring and us just holding on for the victory. The joy of winning a semi-final is immense. At the end Alex, Theo and I hugged each other in delight at the prospect of the cup final. The quality of the match didn't enter our heads, and, in any case, in keeping a clean sheet we had done our job.

The cup final was now our priority. While we were to finish second in the league, realistically we were never going to catch Rangers. We played Airdrie on 10 April, and the game finished 1–1. I was marking Justin Fashanu who scored a wonderful goal that day and we had a really physical battle for 90 minutes. After the game I set off on a marathon trip to Ardgour, on the west coast, where I was speaking. I drove towards Fort William and took a ferry to Ardgour. I spoke at a men's dinner arranged by a local church, stayed overnight and then drove back to Aberdeen via Aviemore on the Sunday.

The 1993 Scottish Cup final was at Parkhead as Hampden was being refurbished. We had a good start to the match but then Rangers scored when I had the misfortune to miskick a clearance. I recovered sufficiently to get in a tackle on Neil Murray, only to deflect the ball into my own net. They got a second when Mark Hateley linked well with Ian Durrant. It was 2–0 at half-time and although Lee Richardson scored late in the game, Rangers managed to hold on for the victory.

The disappointment that I felt after losing to Rangers in the cup final was the most intense that I have ever felt in my football career. At the final whistle I just followed the other lads up the steps but I did not lift my head. I'm not saying this was the right way to handle it; it was just the way it happened.

I came into the dressing-room after the game and said, 'Guys, I'm really sorry.' I felt that the part I had played in the game had actually contributed to losing it. I said, 'I feel I've let the team down and I've let the supporters down.' I just sank on to the seat and put my head in my hands. I was inconsolable.

Some of the lads came over to me and said 'Come on Brian, that's not the case,' and 'Don't be silly, these things happen,' but I just felt disconsolate. The manager wasn't shouting or anything, just disappointed that we'd lost. By the time I eventually got to the showers, most of the others had already gone to the tearoom. Even as I had my shower, I still had this crushing feeling of disappointment that I had never experienced before. There is not much that you can say when you are feeling down. You can't just snap out of it.

It was a real downer on which to finish a good season with Aberdeen. We had finished second in the league, and got to the final of the Skol Cup and the Scottish Cup, each time losing by a single goal as Rangers collected the treble. We went to the Old Course Hotel at St Andrews for our after-match reception with the wives. It was quite a good party despite the disappointment, and at the reception I began to come out of my depression.

The next day we went back to Aberdeen. If we had won it would have been the open-topped bus around the city, but now it was just to Pittodrie. It was raining and it was cold, and I just got into the car and went home. It was the difference between winning and losing; personally, for the team and for the city. I think that is why I took it so badly. I felt worse for the team, the supporters and the city than I did for myself.

For me personally there was still the Estonia game at Pittodrie to come. I reported to the team hotel, the Skean Dhu, on the Monday morning and Andy Roxburgh's first words to me were, 'If you fall down six times, the most important thing is to get up seven times.' It was a challenge for me to get up and be ready to play for Scotland on the Wednesday night, and the very fact that I was preparing for a Scotland game at Pittodrie, probably brought me round a lot quicker than if my season had ended with the cup final. It was a great help too that Andy Roxburgh told me on the Monday that I would be playing in the international.

After the pressure of the cup final the match against Estonia was a really enjoyable game. Winning meant that the season ended on a high for me. I could never have imagined that it could happen.

After that it was great to get away on holiday with the family, and the Monday after my holiday I went to a Christians in Sport meeting of professional footballers in London. It was good to meet other Christian professional players from England like Cyrille Regis and Dennis Bailey. Garth Crooks spoke to us about the importance of pre-season training to prepare you physically for the season, and the similar importance of being prepared spiritually for what God wants us to do. A highlight of the trip was going to the England–Brazil game at Wembley.

I would like to take this opportunity to acknowledge the help that my contacts with the Christians in Sport movement have given me during my football career. At times I have felt quite alone as a Christian in professional football, and meeting other players through the Christians in Sport network has been a great help and encouragement. I would also like to mention Graham Daniels, the assistant director of Christians in Sport, who routinely travels hundreds of miles to spend time with players. He has stayed in our home on more than one occasion, and his visits are a great source of strength to Donna and me.

That weekend with other Christian players helped put the season into perspective for me. The prize that the Rangers captain lifted up would have been nice, and I still feel disappointed that we came second. However, in the Bible we read that the prize that we Christians are aiming for is Jesus Christ, and that is a prize that lasts for ever.

At the time I felt that it would have been better not to have got to the cup final than to have got there and lost, but by the summer the disappointment had subsided. Now I see that while it was disappointing, disappointments are part of life, and it's better to have been part of it than never even to have come close. It was another lesson in football and in life itself. In all parts of my life I aim to remember how much God loves me and how much He wants the best for me. In that context, selfish ambition or jealousy of human achievements by a rival or colleague seem less important.

10

A NEW STAND BUT STILL NO TROPHIES

There was a new atmosphere at Pittodrie with the opening of the Richard Donald Stand behind the goal at the beach end, where the previous season we had played in front of a building site. Princess Anne officially opened the new stand on 18 August when we played Hamburg in a friendly, which was drawn 1–1.

It was another season of so near and yet so far for Aberdeen: second in the league, defeat in the Skol Cup quarter-final after extra time, and a 1–0 defeat in the Scottish Cup semi-final replay. In Europe we lost after being two goals up.

Our pre-season again took us to Holland for three friendlies against Den Haam, Maastricht and Rotweiss from Germany. We won two and drew the other. Holland is often the venue for our pre-season work due to the excellent training facilities on offer and the good quality teams to play against.

I played the first game of the season against Dundee United with Alex McLeish suspended, but was left out for the next one. Having played regularly during the previous season from the Skol Cup final onwards, having scored eight goals and played three games for Scotland, I was pretty disappointed to be left out so early in the season.

I felt that it might have been a reaction to the mistake I'd made in the cup final, and so I was determined to take my chance when I could get it. It soon came, as I was back in for the Skol Cup tie against

Motherwell which was 2–2 at full-time, us winning 5–2 in extra time. I then held on to my place for the season, playing 42 of 44 league games – more than anyone else.

Willie couldn't be faulted for his thoroughness. He enlisted the help of a dietician and a psychologist, to see if this could give us the edge. The psychologist wasn't that well received by the players. He would talk to us just before we went on to the park, trying to relax us and get us to have positive visualisations. But from having all the players in the team taking part in the new pre-match routine, it gradually dwindled to just one or two players left and some of them were doing it because they felt sorry for the psychologist!

Credit goes to Willie for trying it, anyway. His diet plans were well implemented at the club and still are today. Foods which are high in carbohydrate and low in fat are encouraged. After a game the players are now eating jelly babies, liquorice and all sorts of other high carbohydrate sweets. It is a far cry from the days when I first came to Aberdeen when we used to stop at Auchterarder for chip suppers on the way home from away games.

We lost 2–1 to Rangers in the Skol Cup quarter-final after extra time. I conceded a penalty, after 15 seconds of the match. Ian Durrant knocked the ball past me and it was probably going for a goal kick. I was ready to tackle but as the ball was away I didn't go through with it. Durrant went down and from the angle that the referee saw it it probably looked like a penalty, but in fact I made no contact with him. So after less than a minute, Rangers were a goal ahead.

I was stunned but I didn't really react. I didn't say anything to the referee. It is hard to know what to do in those circumstances. If you say nothing it looks like an admission of guilt, yet if you argue with the ref, he won't change his mind and you can be booked for dissent. It really is a no-win situation.

Shortly after this defeat we were off to Glasgow again and managed to beat Celtic 1–0. I always think that after a disappointing result it is good to get in a good win as soon as possible and the win at Celtic did the trick for us.

My next big game was against Switzerland and provided a new experience for me. While the game was at Pittodrie, we were based at Dunkeld House in Perth. It was strange to be on a coach going to play at Pittodrie.

I found in the game against Hibs on the Saturday that I suffered a reaction to the Scotland–Switzerland game. People may find it hard to understand how a fit footballer can have problems playing two or three games in a week. The problem is rarely physical; it is more mental. It is hard to keep your concentration going at the level you need, and in the Hibs game I found I was reacting to things which on a better day I would have been anticipating.

During the years 1992–94 it seemed to me that one big game followed another. I was constantly thinking what a privilege it was to be involved at this level. After the Skol Cup quarter-final it was away to Celtic, then a game for Scotland in the World Cup and then off to Iceland in the Cup Winners' Cup. (With Rangers winning the double and entering the Champions' Cup we, as beaten finalists, were Scotland's representatives in the Cup Winners' Cup.) We won 3–0 over Valur in the national stadium in Reykjavik and, as if that wasn't enough, we followed it by beating Rangers 2–0 at Pittodrie.

Italy was my next port of call – twice in a week in fact. First it was to Rome to play for Scotland against Italy and the following week it was Torino versus Aberdeen in the Stadio del Alpi. We flew to Turin on the Tuesday and trained in the stadium on the Tuesday night. This is common practice in European ties, enabling us to get the feel of the pitch and the atmosphere under the floodlights. We watched Norwich beat Bayern Munich in Germany on TV on the Tuesday night, which gave us a boost and showed us what could be done. On the Wednesday we had a light training session in the morning.

It was an exciting but ultimately disappointing game. We took a 2–0 lead through Mixu Paatelainen and Eoin Jess, playing good quality football which shocked the Italians. Just before half-time Sergio scored with a long shot which rather changed the perspective. In the second half we were constantly under pressure, and desperately trying to hold out. We took off Eoin Jess so we did not have anyone really playing up front. They equalised through Fortunato, but it still looked as if we might hold on for the draw until we conceded a free-kick and the little Uruguayan player Aguilera took it. Scott Booth was in the wall and the ball deflected off him into the net, making it 3–2 to Torino. It was disappointing after such a great start, but I think we would have settled for 3–2 at the kick-off, especially as we had the two away goals.

In the home leg, Lee Richardson scored with a great long shot. At 3–3 we were ahead on away goals. Unfortunately for us Carbone and Silenzi scored one either side of half-time, which meant not only that they were two goals ahead but that they had equalled our away goals; 2–1 and 5–3 on aggregate was how it finished. It had been a European classic. We had lost both games so we couldn't claim that we deserved to win, but still the line between success and failure was a fine one.

The World Cup game for Scotland in Malta in November 1993 was Craig Brown's first in charge. I was picked and we won 2–0, playing a system of three at the back.

Aberdeen had a good 4–0 win over Hibs on 27 November. That night there was a Supporters' Association dinner dance. It is funny how we always seem to have a good win on the day of that event. The previous year it had been 6–2 against Hearts. It's a pity we couldn't have arranged the dinner dance for cup final day, as it might have helped us win!

Our league form continued to be good as we finished second to Rangers. I was in the squad for the Scotland–Holland game, which saw the opening of the new stand at Hampden. Again on that occasion Craig took the time to apologise to me for the fact that I wasn't playing. For me just to be in the squad was more than I could have asked for.

As I watched the Dutch team from the stand I was very impressed with their 'total football'. They were all so comfortable on the ball. The various Dutch players that we have had over the years at Pittodrie have all had that same quality on the ball but there is also a different attitude which is not so suited to the Scottish game. From a time when we used to have six Dutch players in the team we now don't have any. Even Theo Snelders has gone. Nonetheless I am left admiring Theo for his career at the Dons and the way he handled himself in his very difficult last season with us, before a move to Rangers gave him a big boost in the later stages of his career.

In the Scottish Cup we beat East Stirling 3–1 and Raith Rovers 1–0. In the quarter-final we drew 1–1 with St Johnstone, winning the replay 2–0. In the semi-final we met Dundee United. The game was drawn 1–1 but we lost the replay 1–0. We had led 1–0 in the first game, only to concede a last-minute equaliser to take us into a replay. A Jim McInally goal set United up for their final win over Rangers.

The day of the final itself I was in Canada, on tour with the Dons. I remember, standing in a Canadian railway station on our day off, thinking that it would be kick-off time in the cup final back home, and that if we hadn't lost that last-minute goal in the first match I wouldn't be sight-seeing in Toronto, but eagerly looking forward to another crack at Rangers in the Scottish Cup final. Still, Toronto had its compensations, with the CN Tower, the Sky Dome and Blue Jays baseball match and also a visit to nearby Niagara Falls.

The previous year I'd got eight goals and I managed the same number again in 1993–94, mainly through a late burst when I scored against Hearts, Dundee, St Johnstone and Celtic, within the space of 17 days, and each time I got the only goal for Aberdeen. Goal-scoring is always on my agenda. I have scored about 45 goals in first-team matches for Aberdeen. A lot of defenders go up for corners and set pieces but will never cause you a problem unless the ball lands on their head. Others, if the ball isn't right for them, will battle to get a touch so that even if they don't score themselves, they will create something for someone else.

The goal-scoring instinct is something you either have or you don't have. I have always had the desire to score goals and to get involved in the opposition's penalty area. My job is to defend but if I manage to score it is the icing on the cake. It's perfect if I get a goal and we win without conceding a goal, for I've done my job of keeping a clean sheet and also managed to score.

When it comes to shooting chances I will either balloon them or put them in the top corner. You see other players who just clip the ball and hit the target without really troubling the goalkeeper. I am always prepared to make a fool of myself for a chance of scoring.

When you get your first goal of the season it gets you going. The next time you go up for a corner you think, 'I know I can score, perhaps I will again.' Your confidence is up and you are looking for goals and expecting to score. On the other side of the coin, however, if you haven't scored for a year, it is harder to believe you will score today.

During my time at Pittodrie I have scored every season for the first team since I scored in that pre-season friendly in Switzerland in my first season in 1985. From 1992 to 1994 I scored 16 goals in two seasons, a rate that some midfield players would have been happy with. The majority of my goals have been headers, but I've scored more than people might think with my feet. A lot of the important ones have been with the foot; for example, in the cup semi-final against Dundee United. I haven't scored with an overhead kick – yet – but it isn't for want of trying. I did hit the bar against Rangers and the post against Partick with overhead kicks. That is what I mean about being prepared to look foolish for the chance of scoring a goal!

11

SAVED FROM RELEGATION

The 1994–95 season started as usual with pre-season training in July. I was more uptight than normal about my own close-season work and strict diet. I went back weighing 13 stone, a good 12 pounds under weight. However, I sailed through the rigours of running and stamina work and was feeling good as we headed off to Tampere in Finland.

I was just a little concerned by Willie Miller's radical restructuring of the team. Out had gone Alex McLeish to Motherwell as manager, Jim Bett to Iceland and then to Hearts, Lee Richardson to Oldham, Bobby Connor to Kilmarnock and Mixu Paatelainen to Bolton. In had come Billy Dodds from St Johnstone and Colin Woodthorpe from Norwich. Willie was also keen to sign John Inglis from St Johnstone, first mooted in the close season and actually achieved in October. The addition of Peter Hetherston from Raith Rovers and Ray McKinnon from Nottingham Forest made it a very different squad from the team of the previous two seasons when we were consistent in our challenge to Rangers.

Some of the players Willie signed were still living in Glasgow or somewhere in the central belt and only spending part of the week in Aberdeen. That was never the Aberdeen way and somehow at times the new players didn't always seem to have the same commitment to the club as those who had been there for a while.

Having come through the 1994–95 and 1995–96 seasons with their highs and lows, Roy has now instilled in everyone again the need for dedication and professionalism both on and off the park. So while the current team is relatively young, if we can all keep learning and working with each other, then hopefully progress will continue to be made. However, the Old Firm are as strong as at any other time during my years at the Dons and it is all down to money. They have spent and brought top quality players to the clubs and the rest of us have to catch up quickly and not let the Old Firm be dominant. It will be difficult, but it is possible.

Willie wanted us to play with three at the back, supported by two wing-backs, but the team didn't seem to adjust properly to playing the system after years of playing a back four. I felt I was the one who was being left out when it was played, or the one who was substituted during a game if it wasn't working.

Again I wasn't sure why Willie wanted to change the system as over the past year or two we had had the equal best defensive record in the league. I also didn't see why I should be the one to miss out, as I had played with three at the back for Scotland and felt that I was as comfortable with it as anyone else was. Three at the back often means a more simple marking role in defence, and distribution of the ball should always be to an available full-back. As a team we have always struggled with the system. In Jocky and Alex's day an experiment with three at the back was tried but it was very quickly abandoned and the traditional back four restored.

Willie's motivation was positive: second wasn't good enough. I wholeheartedly agree with that but, looking back, I think it was too much change at one time. The press and fans made an issue of using three at the back but Willie was determined to do it his way, and not be influenced by others. I think he persisted too long with it. Ironically, once we had three central defenders in Gary, myself and John Inglis, we never played three at the back until the final two games of season 1995–96. Although we lost 3–1 to Rangers it worked well and in the final match against Falkirk we were comfortable and won the match 2–1. Hopefully, then, it is a good option for the manager to consider in the future.

The first signs of what proved to be a difficult season for me came on that Finnish trip. In our second game, against Tampere, I received a serious gash in the knee. I jumped to head the ball into the net, fell awkwardly and ended up in the back of the net, landing on one of the

In the safe hands of my father the policeman

Counting the cash in the Clydesdale Bank for the last time, as I prepare to move north to join the Dons from Falkirk (© Benny Strain/*Falkirk Herald*)

My first day at Pittodrie – and I had to pinch myself to make sure I wasn't dreaming

Helping out with the Boys' Brigade in the village of Kintore (© D.C. Thomson)

Neil Simpson picking up an award at an Aberdeen Supporters' Club Dinner Dance in 1985, with a young Brian Irvine to help him

14 April 1990: Sheer jubilation as I open the scoring in the Scottish Cup semi-final

My wife Donna and me before a Christmas night out with the other Aberdeen players

Donna and myself launching the Aberdeen College Healthy Eating Campaign

(ABOVE) Never will
forget the momen
when time stood still
scoring the winnin
penalty in the 199
Scottish Cup fina

(LEFT) Theo Snelder
on hand with th
celebration

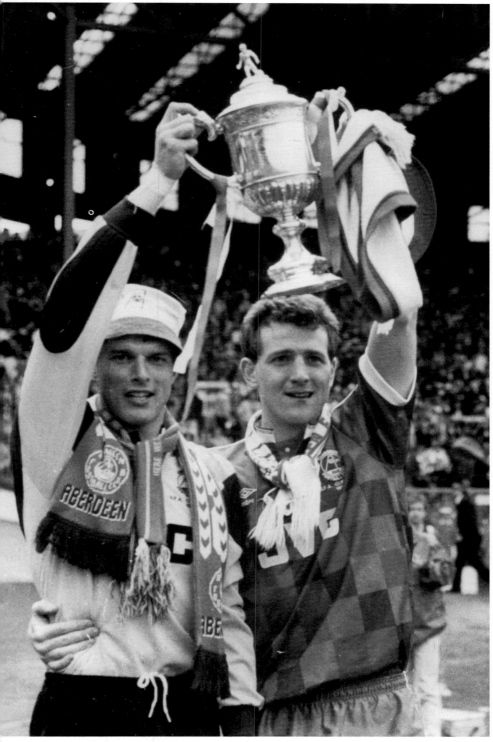

heo and me with the Scottish Cup. Theo's wonderful save from Anton Rogan had
.ade it possible for me to score the winning penalty for Aberdeen

Speaking with Billy Graham in 1991. Sharing my faith at Parkhead and Pittodrie was
great thrill for m

metal hooks on the portable goals. Ironically, the ball would probably have gone in without a touch from me. There was a horrible gash on my kneecap, although I had fortunately avoided damaging the knee-cap itself. As far as I was concerned, the pre-season tour was well and truly 'finn-ished'!

I was desperate to be fit for the first game of the season, so I resumed training as soon as possible and played in the Stewart McKimmie testimonial match against Blackburn, which we won 1–0. However, the knee was not strong and the wound kept reopening. I was delighted to play, though, in my good friend Stewart's special day. He has a tremendous desire to play and has played many a match that others would have missed through injury, so it was fitting for me to have the same attitude in his testimonial.

Brian Grant, Davie Wylie, Teddy Scott and Stewart are the four people who are still there from the time I first joined Aberdeen. Davie Wylie is the physio, or 'the vet' as he is sometimes called by the boys! Joe Miller is also there but he had a spell away with Celtic between 1987 and 1992.

Our first game of the season was a preliminary round tie in the UEFA Cup away to Skonto Riga in Latvia. The ground was no better than many Scottish non-league grounds – hardly the image of European football that one would normally have. Because of the poor facilities we didn't change at the ground but went to and from our hotel in our match strip. I felt a bit awkward to be in a luxurious hotel in what was clearly a very poor and run-down city.

The game had a pre-season feel to it and a 0–0 result was probably acceptable in the circumstances. It could have been better, with new signing Colin Woodthorpe almost scoring at the end. A fortnight later, we were humiliated by the Latvians when we failed to beat them, a 1–1 draw putting them through on away goals. The conditions were difficult, wet and misty, and we failed to create many chances. After an hour the number five board went up. I thought, 'Their number five is being subbed; why isn't he leaving the pitch?' Then I realised that it was me!

I was disappointed to be substituted. I had hardly got my tracksuit on before Skonto scored, ironically through the centre of the defence where I would have been. A late equaliser from Paul Kane was not enough to save us.

That was not the only cup humiliation we suffered that season, as we lost 2–0 to Stenhousemuir in the Scottish Cup. We had struggled in the previous round to beat Stranraer 1–0, which should have acted as a warning to us. That was the game after which Willie came in and smashed the glass panel of the door. It was replaced the following Monday with what I thought was a temporary door, but in fact it is still there today!

My own problems were mounting. I was involved in the Scotland squad for the opening European Championship qualifier against Finland but lost my place for subsequent squads. Craig Brown was marvellous, however, telephoning me the day before the squad for the next match was announced to explain why he was leaving me out. He did not have to do it. The fact that he did just shows the detail into which he goes to do his job so well.

I was also losing my place in the Aberdeen team, as I found myself left out of Willie's teams more and more. My confidence naturally suffered. This was not helped by the continuing press speculation linking John Inglis with Aberdeen. I had spoken to the manager about my desire to stay with the Dons and to commit myself before my contract expired at the end of the season. It was clear, however, that Willie wasn't so keen and when John Inglis signed in October, the storm clouds were gathering on Brian Irvine's horizon. Moreover, I was now having problems with my other knee.

Once John was signed, the club decided that I should go into hospital to have a cyst removed from my knee cartilage. By Christmas I was fit again and challenging for my place, but I was not named in an Aberdeen starting line-up until after Willie Miller was sacked on 7 February. I felt that I did not figure in Willie Miller's plans.

At home things were not easy. Donna was pregnant again and the baby arrived very dramatically, with me just getting Donna to the hospital ten minutes before Christina was born. Like her older sister Hannah, Christina has brought us great joy for which we thank the Lord daily. However, Donna suffered badly from a chronic lack of sleep due to the baby's inability to sleep through the night, and the strain told on both of us. It was the toughest time in our marriage but only strengthened our commitment and love for each other.

Despite my desire to the contrary I was coming to the conclusion that my future at Pittodrie was in real doubt. I phoned the English

PFA and asked for my name to be circulated to clubs in England as a player to be out of contract at the end of the season. It was breaking my heart to think that my time at the Dons was going to finish at the end of the season.

As the club spiralled down the table, the unthinkable relegation was looking more and more likely. We went bottom of the table and looked like staying there. My own involvement was limited to reserve games. In one week I played three reserve games against Partick Thistle, Hibs and Kilmarnock at Armadale, Linlithgow and Troon. This was as low as I have been football-wise in all the years I've been at Aberdeen. I was playing in grounds I used to play in for my junior team, Victoria Park, in the East Lothian League. At times I felt I was back playing at that level again.

Roy Aitken took over as manager and got off to a great start with a 2–0 win over Rangers, but the cup defeat at Stenhousemuir brought us back to reality with a bump. While I was still not in the first team, Roy told me that he expected to offer me a contract at the end of the season. My love for the club, the city and the fans was such that I would have signed just about any contract offered to stay there.

I played against Celtic on 5 March 1995 in a match which we lost 2–0. It was a live TV game and with us in the relegation fight, the stakes were enormous. However, the game turned on one controversial moment. Pierre van Hooijdonk was backing into me. I put my hand out to stop him, and as soon as my hand touched him, he fell down very heavily. I had not pushed him. What is more, the ball went over both our heads so there would have been no reason for me to have fouled him.

I knew that it wasn't a penalty but what was I to do? If I had argued with the referee, I might have been booked or worse. What is more, the TV viewers would be watching to see how I would react. Yet if I said nothing I was effectively accepting the penalty. It was a no-win situation and I felt that all I could do was to say nothing and make a gesture that I had done nothing.

I believe, however, that football has a way of evening things out, and in a later game with Celtic I came back to score. I have found that happen so often in my career. A team or a player gets one over on you, but even if it takes a season for it to happen, you usually get a chance to put the record straight.

Easter proved to be a turning point for me. As a Christian Easter is a special time, when the death and resurrection of Jesus – something which I remember daily – is the focus of one's thoughts in a special way. I was out of the team, my future at the club was uncertain, and Donna and I were stressed and uptight with each other but yet in a marvellous way I had joy and peace in my heart and a deep sense of gratitude to God for His love and care for me. I was able to trust God in a difficult time and to believe that I was not alone with my problems but that God was in control.

On Good Friday Roy told me to keep my head up and that I was a valuable member of the squad. I went to the Good Friday service at the church and on the Saturday went to Pittodrie at 1.30 p.m. for the Celtic game, not expecting to play. On arrival I was told that John had failed a fitness test and that I was playing. The news was unexpected but I was ready to give it everything.

A relaxed pre-match attitude can sometimes help, as at other times I can easily get uptight before a match, as Donna knows only too well. On many Friday nights or Saturday mornings, Donna has learned just to leave me alone.

Well, I gave that Easter game my best goal ever in an Aberdeen shirt in terms of skill. It was a spectacular strike, and all the more enjoyable as seven months of frustration was released in that special moment. It started from a free-kick, and as the ball came across I brought it down with the outside of my right foot. It sat up beautifully, I swung my left foot at it and it flew across Bonner and into the net.

If I was fired up for the start of the match I was now on fire for the remainder of it, and we deservedly won 2–0 to give us some hope on the weekend which reminds us all of the hope we can have in Jesus Christ. For the Christian, knowing that God is in control of everything gives a great sense of security and takes away the worry that so many people feel about the future. As I led the service at Deeside on the Sunday I had real hope in my heart on two fronts – professionally and spiritually.

We played the following Tuesday against my old pal Alex McLeish's team, Motherwell, and despite giving another determined display we lost 2–1 to go back to the bottom. Our misery that night on the journey back north was compounded by news of Dundee United's

3–1 win at Partick to go four points clear of us at the bottom with three games to go. Kate Bush's video to 'Don't give up' was played on the way home in the bus and perhaps reminded us all not to.

We had no match until the following Saturday because of the Scotland qualifier and so we faced Hearts at Tynecastle knowing that defeat would send us down for the first time in our 93-year history. I kept my place despite John's return from injury.

We went one up, only for Hearts to equalise. During the 20 minutes or so that followed we were hanging on by a thread to our place in the league as United were 0–0 at home to Hibs. Then it all swung our way dramatically when Billy Dodds made it 2–1 from a Brian Grant cross. Hearts bombarded us in the final minutes including a free-kick into our box with all their big men up challenging for the ball. We survived and, as we went off, suddenly the large and emotional Dons crowd erupted with news of Hibs scoring in injury time to win 1–0. The gap was down to one point, with the next game at home to Dundee United. We were now on an up, not stopping to think what would happen if we threw it away now, not thinking 'this is scary'. It is only as I look back that I panic and think how frightening it was.

Donna and the girls were packed off to Majorca with her mum and dad for the week. As I ran them to the airport on the morning of the United match I wondered if when they returned to Aberdeen it would still have a team in the Premier League. With Donna's knowledge of football, though, she probably doesn't know the difference between the Premier League and the First Division anyway! Donna calls my training 'work', the fans 'spectators' and the match programme 'the brochure'!

Still, the break was at a good time for us both, giving us space at a tense time when things were still not good between us. Cup finals, Scotland matches, Ibrox, Parkhead . . . none of them could compare with Pittodrie on 6 May. The tension and emotion were tangible. At 3 p.m. every Dons fan held their breath and kicked every ball.

As I came off from my warm-up I gestured to the crowd with my arms and instantly a roar welled around the ground. Every man, woman, boy and girl was up for this one. When we came out at 3 p.m., the fans were incredible. I have never been more proud to wear the Dons' jersey than at that moment, as we took the responsibility of giving the fans what they needed – a place in the Premier League.

The play-offs were the official league matches to stay up, but this was without doubt the 'unofficial' play-off. Remarkably, at this time of year the previous season the same two teams had been playing in the semi-final of the Scottish Cup at Hampden. How the mighty had fallen – but no time for such negative thoughts: on with the action!

We were the team with the bulk of the pressure and Joe Miller crossed beautifully for Eoin Jess. Back to his best, his header was parried only to Billy Dodds to score the first. Just after the hour mark a lovely sweeping move saw Duncan Shearer strike an early shot past O'Hanlon in the United goal, making it 2–0. The fans were already celebrating, leaving the work still to be done to the boys on the park.

However, it would have been too straightforward in this incredible season to win comfortably, and from a corner which was not cleared properly we lost a late goal to give us a long and nervous five minutes to hold on. But we did, and I went off last with Theo, who had just come back into the team after breaking his foot earlier in the season, absorbing this unique atmosphere and trying to convey my thanks to all the fans for such a collective and effective display of support. It crossed my mind after the match that had we lost that day it could have been my last match for the Dons at Pittodrie. To show my love for the Dons I gestured to the fans by attempting to kiss the Aberdeen club badge on my shirt, only to discover later that I had in fact kissed the Umbro badge on the other side of the shirt!

I headed south the next day with a sore leg, very tired but excited about the prospect of sharing the good news of the Lord Jesus with some 8,000 boys at a Boys' Brigade rally at Fir Park. It was great to complete a hat-trick of such events on football pitches, the previous two being in 1991 at Pittodrie and Parkhead with Billy Graham as part of Mission Scotland. Hazel Irvine conducted the interview that day at Fir Park. I knew Hazel previously, but that day confirmed what a professional she is, as well as being a lovely lady. I'm really pleased to see her hosting not just *Sportscene* but also *Grandstand* at times. We discovered we not only share the same surname, but are almost exactly the same age – I am one day older.

The next day, by coincidence, was the anniversary of VE Day, which summed up the mood in the camp. I went down to the beach to watch the fireworks with some friends, but they didn't compare with the fireworks that had been at Pittodrie on Saturday. I had been receiving treatment all week for a balloon-type swelling on my shin, and I got it drained of the blood and fluid that was causing the swelling. There was no way that I was going to miss the Falkirk match.

The rest of the week passed quickly. At home it was very quiet, too quiet, with the three girls, Hannah, Christina and Donna, away on holiday. It was fine for a day or two but then I realised how much I miss them when they are away and I couldn't wait till they were all home again. It is wonderful to have three special ladies in my life now.

A packed house at Brockville awaited us and a good solid 2–0 win ensured that we lived to fight another day. Dundee United were relegated but Motherwell couldn't help us out by beating Hearts, which would have kept us safe in eighth place. Instead a Hearts victory meant that we were still heading for the history books.

Playing in the first ever league play-off, I was a bit worried. The Falkirk game had been a bit of an anti-climax and I hoped that we could retain our vigour for these vital two matches against Dunfermline Athletic. Many felt they were unfortunate not be back in the Premier, having just missed out in past seasons and now missing out on automatic promotion as runners up, as would have been the case previously.

The first leg at Pittodrie went well. Steve Glass scored with a free-kick, but in the second half ex-Don Craig Robertson equalised. It was tense again, but Big Dunc made it 2–1 before I sent him clear late on for a goal and a good 3–1 lead. Now I have to admit that between the Sunday and the second leg on the Thursday I was tense, and frightened we would throw it all away at this last dramatic hurdle. 3–1 sounds comfortable. What if they scored early? What if it finished 2–0, or if it came down to penalties?

By the time Thursday came I was high. As we arrived at East End on a bright early summer's evening, the roads to the stadium were lined with Dons fans. We couldn't let these great fans down, but in the circumstances it added to the tension. We survived early pressure and 0–0 at half-time was satisfactory. Even better was to follow, as we went 2–0 up with goals from Doddsy and Joe Miller. I fell to my knees at the second goal. I had intercepted the ball on the penalty box and broken forward to set up Joe's goal.

The crowd seemed to be more relaxed and were now fully enjoying themselves along with the live TV audience back home in Aberdeen. Again to keep us on our toes, Dunfermline pulled one back to make it 2–1 and 5–2 on aggregate, but it really was a great cushion now and a further goal by young Stephen Glass finished the season in fine style as he dribbled through the Dunfermline defence and around the keeper. Stephen is a lovely, down-to-earth lad who takes everything in his stride and hopefully will have a long and successful career ahead of him. He likes to read footballers' autobiographies so I hope he is reading this one!

I took a twinge of cramp with five minutes to go and was taken off to a fantastic reception from those wonderful fans. As the final whistle sounded the fans released their emotions by invading the pitch and we were told to hurry off. However, the pitch was cleared and we went back out on to the balcony to cheer and thank our heroes – whilst they did the same to us. I gave my shirt away to a good friend from church, Louise Macklin, whom I saw in the crowd. She has framed it and put it on the wall in her son's bedroom.

Teddy Scott, the man who amongst other jobs looks after the kits, got hold of me the next morning and gave me a row for my shirt being missing from his laundry bag. Teddy has a lovely way of keeping your feet firmly on the ground. But equally, he is always there for players, young and old, to encourage and guide them. He is a tremendous servant to Aberdeen.

It has been my privilege to know Teddy, and to be helped through the years by him. He has lots of jobs to do at the club and he gets on with his work quietly, without looking for the recognition that players tend to look for in their careers. He puts in tremendous hours in a totally reliable and dedicated way, and has been a big influence in the club over the years. Ask any past or present player about Teddy Scott and I'm sure everyone would recall a special man. The story goes that when he forgot to pack the away strips for a pre-season match, Alex Ferguson said, 'Right that's it – Teddy's getting the sack,' whereupon Gordon Strachan piped up, 'Well that's ten jobs up for grabs!'

One incident in particular stands out in my own mind, exemplifying the type of man he is. In July 1995 whilst unable to train because of the illness, I was sitting in the empty dressing-room with the boys all out at pre-season training. I was reading through the hundreds of letters I'd received after the news of my illness was made public. One letter from a man, no doubt well-meaning, was telling of how devastating MS had been to his wife, and told me in great detail what had gone wrong. This was too much for me to take, especially as I was just coming to terms with things myself and I started to cry.

Not wanting to make a scene I sat in the dressing-room with my head down, sobbing quietly but feeling that I had to let the tears come flooding out in order to feel better. Teddy, seeing me upset, took my arm and led me to his room, an Aladdin's cave of kit and equipment, covered from wall to wall with pennants and old pictures of the Dons – well worth a visit if you ever get a tour of Pittodrie! He sat me down at a desk and came back a few minutes later with a cup of tea with two sugars and said simply, 'Here you are, Brian.' He gave me the tea and offered me a biscuit from his biscuit tin and said, 'Take your time and you'll be all right.' Simple, sincere words and sure enough it did the trick. He didn't need to say anything or try to be clever with words. His actions and calmness did it all.

Back to East End Park, and the dressing-room was a happy and relieved place. The 1994–95 season, which had been a terrible season for the club and for myself, on the whole had finished on a glorious high. We hadn't won anything but to get out of our dire position in the league was a real achievement. Perhaps I felt those storm clouds were clearing slightly and there was some sunshine breaking through at last. A new contract and the skies would be blue, I thought.

When we arrived back in Aberdeen later that evening the boys went out for some drinks, but I headed for the Dolphin chip shop and in the small café just off Union Street sat down with the owner Graham Herd to a black pudding supper, tea and bread and butter. It was a late-night feast I thoroughly enjoyed, and though it is not the orthodox way for a footballer to celebrate a good result, this was my way. I got home around 2 a.m. but didn't sleep a wink all night.

It was very strange, and because of a Barnardo's charity dinner the next night that I attended as a guest along with, among others, Alex Ferguson, it was fully 41 hours that I went without sleep from the Thursday morning at 8 a.m. till 1 a.m. on the Saturday morning after the dinner. A family wedding reception the next day added to the tiredness, and by the Monday I was glad of a hospital stay to explore my knee for the cyst which, it was discovered, was now clear.

Yes, the blue skies were here and I headed off on my mini-tour of Scotland to share my faith, feeling the pressure of work completely lifted for the first time in nine months. As I drove in the car from Grantown-on-Spey to Perth and on to Stirling, little did I know what the frightening outcome of a strange tingling sensation in my foot was to be.

By early June, as I prepared to go off to some speaking engagements around the country, I spoke to Roy about a new contract and very quickly agreed to one for a further two years. I signed the contract on Monday 12 June. Later that day Donna and I went off to Cameron House Hotel for a relaxing two days on our own to celebrate. However, the strange feeling in my feet was still there and I didn't know what it was. Once home the next day, I phoned my doctor. I couldn't believe how quickly he was moving to arrange for me to go into hospital for tests.

The blue sunny skies were to turn darker than ever and the storm of recent times was nothing compared to the one ahead.

12

THE DAY THE WORLD STOPPED

The storms may come but they can never turn back the person whose heart is in touch with the Lord, and the eye of the storm is calm and peaceful and clear whilst all around is dark, stormy and violent. I feel these illustrations describe my position in the summer of 1995. I make no apology that the account of that period of my life is at times a bit emotional. I have sought simply to tell it like it was.

I had a persistent tingling sensation in my foot and it did not appear to be going away. A few days after I'd signed my new contract I went to my doctor who seemed a bit concerned and sent me to Foresterhill Hospital for tests and treatment. Strange, I thought. But nonetheless I was glad something was being done to clear the foot problem up quickly, or so I thought.

When I checked into Ward 40 the specialists did a lumbar puncture where a long, and I mean long, needle went in somewhere in my lower back to take fluid out of my spinal cord. What surprised me was that the doctor made his diagnosis without seeing the results of the lumbar puncture. He felt the symptoms I was describing were conclusive in themselves: I had multiple sclerosis.

Anyway, after a day of tests on the Thursday I was put on a course of steroids, which were taken intravenously for three days. I was feeling pleased, in total ignorance, thinking this would clear up the problem and it would be all right. However, after the weekend passed, the doctor came into my ward and started explaining how he felt that in time these sensations should settle down and hopefully everything would be back to normal. Although he had never treated a professional sportsman, I should be able to continue as before.

At this point I was a bit suspicious as to why he should mention my career and the fact that things should be okay. But worse was to follow. 'I cannot say how long it will take to clear,' he said. 'It is likely to clear, but how long I don't know.'

'Oh dear,' I remember thinking, 'It's only 5–6 weeks till pre-season. I hope it clears up by then, to get going for the new season.' Then he mentioned one or two other points and with these thoughts in my head I was distracted from his general line of talk until I heard the words 'multiple sclerosis'.

He continued speaking, then paused. 'You don't seem surprised,' he said. 'Is that what you thought yourself?' I said that it wasn't at all what I had thought. He spoke on of what I've no idea – then left the room and closed the door. I was sitting on the bed alone when it suddenly hit me. My pulse raced. I felt hot. I felt claustrophobic. I thought I was going to be physically sick. My eyes were full of tears. I prayed to the Lord to be close, and to be my strength.

It was like someone saying, 'You're dying but it's not as bad as it sounds.' I understood the seriousness of multiple sclerosis but I couldn't relate my symptoms to something that could have finished my career.

The nurse came into the room and tried to help. They ran me a bath which I jumped out of straight away, feeling that I was going to drown lying in it. My wife and friends started arriving. The door to my ward was closed with an official notice on it, not allowing visitors without permission. Donna and I had been unprepared for this. Friends had been suspicious but we just weren't expecting anything like this label on my condition. I looked out of the window over the city to the North Sea, and there, right in the midst of the buildings, was Pittodrie in all its splendour.

Everyone who arrived to see me was greeted in the same emotional way of uncontrolled tears and the inability to speak for the initial ten minutes or so. Strangely, I was strong with Donna and tried to make sure she wasn't unnecessarily upset in addition to the shock she was obviously in. Douglas Smith, George Adams, John and Sheena Bevan and Carol Rankin – each of these Christian friends were there at the right time in the right way. These and others at subsequent times in the months ahead demonstrated clearly what it means to be brothers and sisters in the Christian family and made God even more real to Donna and me at this traumatic time.

George Adams was a great comfort when he visited me, reminding me that the Lord's prayer says 'Thy will be done' and that I had to accept God's will, not my own. George could speak with some authority here, having lost his own Aberdeen career through injury.

John Bevan worked in the hospital and he often used to call in to see how I was. One day, Brian Wilson was in to visit me. Instead of cheering me up, he could only show how upset he was and we were both crying. Just at that moment John walked in and said, 'How are you doing?' I replied, 'I'm having a good day, John' – which had been true up to the point that Brian and I had got upset. When John said, 'Well I wouldn't like to see you on a bad day!', the three of us just burst out laughing.

John's wife Sheena came round and talked to Donna and me to help us cope with the problems that the illness caused. In May 1996 Sheena sent me this note, which was a great encouragement:

'Just a note to let you know how thrilled we are that you have reached the end of the season strong and in such good form. We have remembered you many times in our prayers and thank God for the strength that He has given you.

You have come so far over the past year. God has really been working in your life. I go back to a heart-breaking conversation with you in hospital last year, which I know at the time was difficult.

I really don't know why we have to go through such dark painful times but we have to believe that God can and will use these situations and I believed then and still do that God is not finished with you yet, Brian. The best is yet to come!

Those who wait on the Lord will renew their strength.'
What a difference a day makes!

I was discharged from hospital a week after I had been admitted and the world seemed a different place from the one I had left a week earlier. We moved quickly to book up a week's stay at the Craigendarroch Lodges in the lovely Royal Deeside village of Ballater.

Up until that point the summer had been cold and cloudy but in the weeks and even months that followed we had sunny blue skies to help heal our hurt and upset. For such a low point in our lives, Ballater was a special and memorable holiday which lasted not one week as planned, but three glorious weeks. I say glorious, but obviously it was still a very emotional time, and at night whilst the family was asleep I would slip upstairs in the lodge and cry my eyes out and pray to my Lord as never before.

We all want to enjoy life, yet pleasure and Christian joy cannot be equated. Pleasure depends on circumstances, whereas Christian joy is completely independent of any such circumstances. Pleasures come and go. The joy of God is constant. Pleasures are superficial. Joy is deep. It wells up from inner contentment. Godly joy is not something a Christian is required to have, but rather a consequence of having been set free from the bondage of sin and knowing that one's feet are on the road that leads to the Father's house – Heaven. We don't have to acquire joy. It comes to us when we experience salvation, of its own accord. This truth, this fact, kept me going in these dark nights.

Two poems were very helpful at this time:

> Trusting in His love in days of trial,
> Even though the prospect looks so drear;
> Knowing well the Lord never breaks His word,
> And though now unseen is ever near.
> All that comes to me is His good purpose,
> Though the good I may not see;
> Any path that God in wisdom chooses
> Is the right way home for me.
>
> Worry not, my dearest son;
> Don't you know you are my beloved one?
> All I ask is that you trust in me
> And from your troubles I will set you free.
>
> There is a troubled frown upon your face;
> Come to me child, I will bring you solace.
> Your eyes show your fear –
> Don't you know at times like this I am very near?

Turn to me in all your sorrow,
Don't worry about tomorrow.
My dearest child, my love is true;
Trust is all I ask of you.

When I was in Perth on the day I first had a tingling sensation in my foot, I spoke at a men's outreach supper held by the men of Tayside Christian Fellowship. They had a game of football at the astroturf pitch at McDiarmid Park, St Johnstone's ground, with their friends and colleagues from work. Afterwards they came back to the church where a meal was served and then I was interviewed and shared my faith and details of my football.

At the end one chap in the audience asked me what my favourite scripture verse was. I don't have a particular favourite but somehow, I don't know why, I thought of *Romans 8:28* 'And we know that all that happens to us is working for our good if we love God and are fitting into his plans.' Billy held up a leaflet he had in front of him and it contained the same verse. It wasn't so obvious that night but in the days, weeks and months that have followed, that verse has been a source of supreme comfort, hope and confidence that God is always in control, and His way and will is best.

Also, on the speaking tour which had taken me to Perth and Stirling I had twice seen the same tapestry of the Last Supper. The next time I was to see it was in the hospital chapel at Foresterhill. It spoke of what the Lord was about to go through the night before Calvary and let me know that my Saviour had been through an ultimate sacrifice and time of suffering, and that His suffering and sacrifice ended in victory and eternal life for all His followers.

This is my trust. This is my hope. This is the God on whom I depend each and every day. In the chapel I prayed and sat alone and, as well as seeing the tapestry for the third time, as I left, I noticed the open Bible beside the door. The page it was opened at was *Romans 8*, and of course verse 28 spoke to me again.

Back in Ballater we were enjoying ourselves. The weather, at the start of a long hot summer, was glorious. Deeside is a lovely spot and in beautiful summer weather there are not many better places in the world. Just along from our holiday lodge the River Dee ran past and on a lovely Sunday evening I sat alone with my feet in the water surrounded by natural beauty and splendour. The sky was blue, the air clear and everything was calm and tranquil, except for the water gently rushing downstream. The *23rd Psalm* was so relevant to me that night and once again I was in tears, but not with sadness. Joy and peace were bubbling up in my heart and I wished the moment could last forever.

Psalm 23

'The Lord is my shepherd; I have everything I need; He lets me rest in meadow grass and leads me beside the quiet streams. He gives me new strength. He helps me do what honours Him the most.

'Even when walking through the dark valley of death I will not be afraid, for you are close beside me guarding, guiding all the way. You provide delicious food for me in the presence of my enemies. You have welcomed me as your guest. Blessings overflow. Your goodness and unfailing kindness shall be with me all of my life, and afterwards I will live with you forever in your home.'

Some readers may find it strange the way I keep quoting the Bible and may be wondering what relevance an old book could have to a practical situation. As a Christian I believe, of course, that the Bible is not merely an old book but is God's Word. At a time when, in human terms, my outlook was bleak, it was a great comfort to me to be able to focus on the eternal dimension. While my short-term future may have been uncertain, the certainty that I would spend eternity with God put it all in perspective.

Also throughout this book I have often spoken about prayer. For those who are not aware of the power of prayer, it is something that is very real indeed and extremely powerful. It is also one of the ways in which God can talk to us. Again, you may ask, 'How can God talk?' In my experience I have heard God's words to me in several ways. One is through the character of Jesus. Whatever Jesus did whilst he lived on earth as a Christian I should do the same. Ever since the Bible came alive to me I have heard God's word to me in the Bible itself, but also through circumstances. For example, when one door closes and another opens, it is clear that God is guiding me in these situations.

Finally, I have heard God speak through the direct whispering of the Holy Spirit within me, although wisdom is needed to discern between the voice of God's Holy Spirit and my own voice telling me what to do.

The week in Ballater quickly passed but we were enjoying the holiday so much that we ended up staying for three weeks. By now my close friend Douglas and his family were up for a summer break in Ballater too, and we enjoyed each other's company, going to beautiful spots along the Deeside route in quite glorious weather.

Occasionally I would get quite down when any physical exertion left me feeling a bit strange in the legs. But Doug was great in that I wasn't allowed to feel sorry for myself. I actually started to feel better – perhaps the steroids I received in hospital were having a short-term effect – and we started going for long walks, round the picturesque Loch Muick, the Seven Bridges of Ballater and up the Craigendarroch Hill which offers beautiful views of the Dee Valley and Ballater itself to marvel at.

As July 12 came, the pre-season return date, I wasn't anywhere near the stage to resume training and that was a frustration. But I thought perhaps another couple of weeks, and I hoped to resume without anybody having to know publicly of my diagnosis.

So far I haven't mentioned the impact that all this had had on Donna. Following the stress of the previous year and the difficulties we had been having with Christina's inability to sleep through the night, I feel that it was equally devastating to Donna's life. She has been very brave and supportive to me throughout, but like me she had a good few nights at Ballater where she had to let her emotions go and let the tears flow.

We brought some problems on ourselves when we went to the local library and got a book entitled *MS and How to Cope*. As you might imagine, it left us feeling very low as it described mainly how to cope with the worst scenarios. You can imagine just how helpless and afraid Donna really was. However, the shock and trauma of summer 1995 has begun a real healing process in our relationship, that had been affected by the stresses and strains of everyday life. I am so thankful that as the weeks, months and, I pray, years unfold, there is a real healing process going on in our lives, both physically and spiritually.

Christian unity exists between Christians so, obviously, it exists between Donna and me. It is the bond between one person and another, which enables us to know that the things that unite us are deeper and more important than the things that might separate us. Going back to what you read earlier about our first date, my lack of dress sense was not so important as the Christian faith that we shared! More seriously, it is the same principle through all the difficulties Donna and I face, like any Christian couple. We have the bond of Christian unity in our lives and in our marriage.

All good things must come to an end, and the holiday was sadly over. We benefited from it immensely however, and it gave us a much-needed break especially bearing in mind what lay ahead. In a matter of weeks it became clear that the illness could not be kept quiet. I was treated in a public hospital on an open ward, although I had my own room, and it was very quickly being rumoured that I had MS.

In July I was not going into training but just going out for walks. I could manage only two miles. The official story at that time was that I had a trapped nerve in my back which was causing pain down my legs. It was true as far as it went but it was anything but the whole truth.

Rumours aren't quite so bad if you can get back to playing quickly and dispel them, but this obviously wasn't going to happen. Also, one or two people had actually said to me that they had heard what was wrong. It was beginning to get me down and naturally at this time I wasn't too strong. It was hard even to organise simple household chores and duties, so the whole idea of being a potential major news item was a burden which I felt I could not face.

However, I was finding keeping the lid on everything quite a strain. I was wondering about going to the press. I was recommended to approach a journalist, Frank Gilfeather, for advice on how to go public with the story. I wasn't in the best state of mind to handle things like this and I was keen to get the story out without it being sensationalised. Frank's advice was to offer the story to one paper and he suggested the *Daily Mail.*

When he approached the *Daily Mail* they were very keen to have the story on an exclusive basis. They saw it as a real scoop. Gradually I became more uneasy about all this and my friend Doug acted on my behalf. After long phone calls to the *Daily Mail* on Sunday night, we persuaded them not to run the story on the Monday morning.

This three-way telephone conversation between Douglas, me and the *Daily Mail* took place at the house of some friends, Phil and Carol

Rankin. When the calls were over for the night Donna and I just broke down in tears. Phil took the children – our two and their three – outside to play while Carol calmed us and tried to console us.

I remember that Carol prayed such a lovely, sincere prayer for us as we all kneeled on the floor with tears flowing from our eyes. It was a great help to give our problem to God and to draw on His strength, and once again it was great to be surrounded by such loving and caring friends.

We also persuaded the club that the time had come to end the rumours and speculation by making a public statement. I made the following short statement at the normal Monday press conference at the club. It obviously caught the press totally unawares.

> Earlier this summer, after undertaking some tests in hospital, I was diagnosed as having MS. I am in a positive frame of mind. I am in the recovery process. I have been assured by medical experts that I will be able to resume training shortly and be back to full fitness and playing very soon thereafter.
>
> This has been a difficult time for my family and myself and I am indebted to Aberdeen Football Club and all those in the medical world who have been so helpful and understanding. I am so grateful for my faith in the living God at this time.

Just before it was read to the press I got the club doctor, Derek Gray, to read it out to my team-mates in the dressing-room. They were all naturally very shocked, but although I had only shared it with close colleagues like Stewart McKimmie, most others had already heard the rumours.

By the time I arrived home there were half a dozen photographers at the front door with reporters. I said I had nothing to add to the statement but the photographers explained they had to wait for as long as it took for a picture for the next day's papers. So I was pictured outside the house pretending to read the statement I had just made.

The ones who stayed and hid just round the corner for further pictures and any other words were in for a long wait as Donna and I slipped out the back and were picked up by a friend at the bottom of our garden which is secluded with tall, thick trees. We spent the next couple of days at Donna's parents to escape from the unwanted visitors.

The next day's papers were full of the story and though I have no complaint, it was very distressing to read of what might happen, what has happened to somebody else and so on. But that was because I was reading about something that was raw and painful just then. I felt desperately for both sets of parents, relatives and friends, who would either be finding out for the first time themselves or, as in our parents' case, facing the burden they now had of answering their friends' questions. All in all, this was the most traumatic time, even more so than the time the doctor's diagnosis was made during my stay in hospital.

I was overwhelmed by the level of interest in the announcement. It made the front page of many of the papers. The *Press and Journal* even referred to me in its editorial: 'Aberdeen footballer Brian Irvine has announced that he suffers from multiple sclerosis, but expects to make a full recovery. Brian is positive and optimistic and insists that he will carry on playing the game he loves. Such an attitude at what must be a stressful time is commendable, and will surely inspire others who have been given similarly bad news but who are much more apprehensive about the outcome.'

I later gave an interview to the *Press and Journal*, which was printed on 26 July. The article gives a good summary of what I was feeling at that time:

> The first thing I want to make clear is that this interview is the first I have given since I found I had MS – apart from the brief statement I read out at Pittodrie on Monday – which is intended for publication.
>
> The reason I am speaking to the *Press and Journal* is that I want to let the Aberdeen fans know how I feel after hearing the news and hope that I can make clear just what the problem is.
>
> I could hardly take it in when I went into Aberdeen Royal Infirmary about seven weeks ago for tests after feeling ill with back pain and weakness in my legs, and was told I had MS.
>
> Multiple sclerosis is a name which sends fear through people and I was totally unprepared for it. But though my wife, Donna, and I were devastated to hear the news we were heartened to hear that it was a mild form, and that I have a great chance of recovering completely.

116

Probably the most difficult thing for me after that was not being able to tell people I had the condition when they would ask me how I was. I know the club had to say something when I was not appearing at pre-season training and it was described as a back problem, which was true in a sense since my back was affected.

I thought long and hard about how to make the situation public and finally decided, with the club's help, to read a prepared statement and hope that it would be left at that. Perhaps I should not have been surprised to read in the papers descriptions of MS at the extreme end of the spectrum, right up to situations where people were said to die from it.

That's understandable, I suppose, for the disease has a vast range, but I believe the specialists who have told me that the likelihood is that I should be able to make a full recovery, and perhaps not be bothered by it again. The main problem seems to be inflammation that attacks the nerves and goes via the back down to the legs. But rest calms the inflammation down and, rather like a virus, it goes into remission and recovery begins.

That means I can then start to rebuild the muscles, since I am obviously out of condition without pre-season training, and work my way steadily back to fitness.

The degree of the illness I appear to have might not have been highlighted so much but for the fact that I am in a high profile situation as a professional footballer and in a game where the body is punished through training. For many people the mild form I have, especially if they were involved in sedentary jobs, would mean they did not have to miss even a day at work.

There are 8,000 sufferers in Scotland and the severity shows a wide variance. But even in quite serious cases, where people have had to spend time in a wheelchair, they have remission times when they can walk about quite freely.

Of course I am well aware that even if, as I hope and pray, I recover completely from this attack, there is no guarantee that it will not come back at some future time. But none of us has a guarantee of perfect health in the future. People have serious accidents or fall ill with a variety of ailments, so I'm no different from them. Professional footballers have to live with the fact that the punishing sport they are in can lead to arthritis in the future and give them a pain-filled existence when they finish playing.

My belief in the living God means that I will look on the positive side and think about getting back to good health. I am very lucky to be married to Donna and have two wonderful daughters, Hannah and Christina.

Aberdeen is a special club and I regard myself as being fortunate to have nine international caps as well as being with a club I want to continue playing for.

I hope the fans get a clear picture of how I feel about the situation and now that I have cleared the air I hope to be left to concentrate on a full recovery and do my talking on the next occasion where it matters – on the football field.

When the announcement was made it was a help to have it out into the open. It did, however, bring a pressure of its own. I got a great number of letters, most of which were helpful and encouraging, but some people would write and tell me that they had a friend who had MS and he died! I read all the letters and tried to take it all in, but even getting letters saying 'I'm really sorry to hear . . .' had the effect of making me feel down and sorry for myself. Many of the letters I received from all over the country had the same disturbing effect on me. I could be depressed for the rest of the day after reading them, even though I knew that they had been sent with good intentions.

Whenever I came out of the door at home or Pittodrie or wherever I went, there were people coming up to me and saying how sorry they were to hear about my illness. There is nothing positive that can come from having people constantly offering their condolences to you, but I tried not to develop negative thoughts.

Donna and I were also hitting a low in our relationship. On the Tuesday before the first match of the season, I phoned a friend, Geoff Norrie, and arranged to go to the cinema. I had packed an overnight bag and said to Donna as I left the house that I wasn't coming back!

We went to the film *The Englishman who went up a hill and came down a mountain* starring Hugh Grant. As I walked with Geoff from the car to the cinema, I had the terrible feeling in my legs which restricted me to a very slow pace. I was filled with mental anguish at being so limited as I walked such a short distance. After the film I said goodbye to Geoff and decided to book into a hotel for the night.

When I woke up the next morning I thought I would extend this period of 'escape' and went to my good friend Yens Arpes, a German, who is general manager of the Skean Dhu Hotel at Altens in Aberdeen's outskirts. I explained to Yens, who is a terrifically hospitable man, that I was in need of time on my own due to all the pressures of the past weeks.

The third floor of the hotel was being refurbished and I was able to stay in a newly refurbished room which wasn't yet available for use to the public. I settled in, bought some food and decided to 'camp out' for a few days of hard thinking. However, I didn't explain to Donna where I was going and although she felt sure I had done just what I was doing, when I didn't phone or get in touch she got more than a bit worried.

On the Wednesday, I had an appointment with the consultant who had treated me in June. As I walked through the hospital grounds on a glorious sunny day, there lying in the sun on the grass outside the maternity hospital was my cousin Marie Middleton.

Marie was always a cousin I was close to in our younger days. She had been expecting her first child that summer, but had the baby extremely prematurely and the chances of baby Amy surviving were not great. Now some eight weeks later Marie was still at Aberdeen Special Nursery with the baby. As we sat on the grass we encouraged one another in this desperate situation for us both (and our spouses). We wiped our tears and went on our way, and thankfully Amy is going strong and we have moved on from that dark day in brilliant sunshine.

After the routine visit to the doctor I went back to the hotel and stayed in the room, made something to eat, spent some time reading and then watched TV before going to sleep. By now, with lots of time to think, I was reaching a crucial attitude of mind. Up till now, I had been dwelling on all that I couldn't do just now and feared I wouldn't be able to do in the future. I now realised that, whatever I was to be like, it was vital to think and concentrate on what I could do – both now and in the times ahead.

Thursday passed quietly in my room and I phoned a hairdresser who came to the room and cut my hair very short – a style I never had before. It was somehow a statement of how I felt inside. By Friday I reported to Pittodrie, unable to do anything except dwell on the agony of missing out on tomorrow's big kick-off. Once at Pittodrie I decided for some reason, I don't know why, to phone Doug, and when I did I very quickly realised the panic I had caused. I met Doug and went for lunch with him at the beach. Being the friend he is, he just listened, instead of criticising me for being so foolish by leaving no word of where I was.

As I look back the idea of going away was right but not telling Donna where I had gone was wrong. By the second night away, and with some friends phoning to see how I was after my visit to the doctor and being told by Donna I was 'missing', the panic had set in. Doug spent a large part of Thursday evening driving around town looking for either me or my car, to no avail. I felt the break had worked as I now had a much more determined and positive attitude to the situation and was only sorry I had caused so much anxiety with my disappearance.

I still hadn't seen Donna but I phoned her on Friday night and though we were still unhappy with each other we arranged a 'date' for Saturday night. Donna's mum and dad were to look after the girls.

What was now in my mind I had felt the Lord speaking to me, adding to the verse in *Romans 8:28*. I read in my daily Bible reading notes: 'Disappointments, when seen in the light of eternity, become "His-appointments". God takes the obstacles and turns them into opportunities. He marches in through the door of every disappointment to bring something out of it which is good.'

So if the 'time side' of life is a bit rough at the moment, then let the 'eternity side' hold you steady. Something good comes out of disappointment – you'll see. Because of the letters I was receiving each day by the hundred, I was aware that both Christians who knew me and those who only knew of me were praying for me and this was bringing great encouragement, not just to me but also to Donna in all our troubles.

Another Bible verse which helped me at this time was *2 Corinthians 1:11*: 'But you must help us too by praying for us, for much thanks and praise will go to God from you who see His wonderful answers to your prayers for our safety.' I trusted God to encourage those who were praying and those who would see the results in my recovery.

When I eventually got back home and settled ready for the fight ahead I started taking it one step at a time. I got back to walking each day, not as before in the lovely scenery of Deeside, but along the often cold and windy front on Aberdeen beach. I went from Pittodrie to Footdee and back in an hour, then in 55 minutes, then 50. Then I was jogging the last bit. Then jogging a bit more until I was eventually jogging the whole way.

At first I was left with a buzzing in my lower back and top of my legs for half an hour or so, then it would be 25 minutes, then 20. Eventually the buzzing was gone in five minutes. Gradually during that two to three week period I was able to do more and more and feel fewer and fewer after-effects.

Still the public support grew and I am so grateful to the Aberdeen fans and public who have taken me into their hearts more than ever with the news of my illness. I have said before that Aberdeen is the only team I ever dreamt as a boy that I could play for, and I have been the Dons' fans' representative on the pitch in all the games I've played.

At the first match of the new season, a conversation with one of the stewards who helps on match days in the main stand was to prove a moment of great significance. He had suffered from ME and had been unable to work for a year. He asked me how I was doing and told me about a Rosalie Dickinson, who had him back on his feet within a month. He gave me the address and I said I'd contact her.

After the match I went back to the hotel and waited for Donna to come. I looked out of the window to the road to see Donna arrive, and car after car passed before she eventually arrived. We went for a meal in the restaurant and talked through some of the difficult times we had been going through. We decided I would stay another night at the hotel and I went home later on the Sunday. I went to a church in town on my own and went back home ready to face the future that lay ahead both on and off the field.

One important truth I have learnt over the past few months is that life is really all about relationships – our relationship with God and relationships with others. Love and respect for people must be at the centre of all our work if we are Christians. Ambitions, possessions, and so on mean nothing in comparison. I came to recognise that everything I have is a gift from God and I was grateful for it.

The problem now was that I was receiving so many letters from people with suggestions about cures and remedies that I was a bit sceptical about yet another one, but I phoned the number the steward had given me. They had a three-month waiting-list but, because of the press coverage, they knew who I was and were prepared to see me. About two weeks later I was able to get an appointment with Rosalie, after which I started to improve.

Rosalie Dickinson is a remarkable lady whom I found to be very perceptive and, above all, very helpful on my road to recovery. At the clinic they treat the cause of the symptoms that they have discovered using mineral, vitamin, herbal and, if needed, homeopathic treatments. The test they carry out is complicated to explain but it produces incredibly accurate diagnoses, suggesting subsequent treatments. Rosalie has practised for 15 years and as she says, 'the proof of the pudding is in the eating'. She has many successfully treated patients with a long waiting-list for new patients.

Rosalie's tests indicated that a polio vaccine that I received as a child, coupled with a vaccine against whooping cough and scarlet fever, had caused a reaction within the spinal cord. It had, she felt, been under the surface for years. One suggestion as to what had triggered this illness was that the traces of vaccine within me had combined with a virus and this, coupled with the stress that I was under over a period of two years, brought things to a head in 1995.

Rosalie pin-pointed times when this should have made me feel unwell and when I checked the dates I had to agree with her. There was a time when the virus had affected the labyrinth in the hearing canal. She asked if I had had any problems about two years ago, and I could look back to a time when I had a kind of vertigo when I would sit down and the whole room would spin round. She also pin-pointed February the year before, and again I had been having severe headaches which I had just put down to the stress of the relegation battle. Once again she had been right.

The stress that I was under during that period had certainly not helped. However, to be told a specific cause for the illness was a lot more helpful than being told by the doctors that they did not know how or why it had happened or what the future would hold.

When Rosalie diagnosed the problem and started to give me treatment, it was in the form of minerals and vitamins, rather than drugs. Herbal antibiotics were used to boost the body's immune system. The treatment that she has given me has certainly triggered the recovery, for it was only after I had gone to see her that I was able to resume training. By coincidence, Braco, where Rosalie lives, is just a few miles from where the tingling sensation started in my feet when I was speaking in the summer at Perth and Stirling.

The first time I went to Rosalie, Donna and the girls came with me and went to the shops in Perth. When I met them afterwards, before I said anything Donna asked, 'What's happened?' She picked up immediately that my mood was different. I believe that in response to the prayers of thousands of Christians who were praying for me, God led me to the right person for the right treatment. I think that whatever caused the original outbreak is still there but if through the minerals and vitamins I am able to keep my body above a certain level then Rosalie has every confidence that I will remain as healthy as I am now.

So, having been to Rosalie and now starting light jogging, I was experiencing the attitude of being 'quietly confident' in prospects. Doug and I would use 'QC' as our catchphrase. Doug would say, 'QC?' 'Yes, QC,' I would reply. I would say to myself, 'Quietly confident in God, now and always.' I now had another verse which gave me strength, from *1 Peter 5:10*: 'The God of all grace who called you to His eternal glory in Christ after you have suffered a little while will Himself restore you and make you strong, firm and steadfast.'

When I went to the hospital in November, the doctor who treated me told me that the recovery I had made was such that he did not want to see me again and hoped that he would never see me again. I had expected that he would want to keep monitoring me, so I was greatly encouraged by this. At one stage I probably thought about the illness 500 times a day. Now it is much less. Beforehand, of course, I didn't really know what MS was, and to some extent the doctors themselves don't understand it fully.

Another Bible passage which gave me encouragement was *Psalm 40:1-3*: 'I waited patiently for the Lord. He turned to me and heard my cry. He lifted me out of the slimy pit, out of the mud and the mire. He set my feet on a rock and gave me a firm place to stand. He put a new song in my mouth, a hymn of praise to our God. Many will see and fear and put their trust in the Lord.' What God has done in my life in these recent times speaks louder than any of my words in the past. Actions do speak louder than words.

It was great to have Donna's mum and dad, Donald and Irene Main, living so close to us when things were hard. Their support was tremendous. Another friend who has been helpful was Fiona Cordiner, a dietician who advised me on my diet and gave much practical help as I recovered from the illness.

What the last year has taught me is that God's family is a reality. The importance of belonging to God's family and the help and support that that brings has been a great help to me. The reality of the love and support of so many Christians has been for me proof of the reality of God in so many practical situations.

Another illustration which helped me was this. A young child was about to have an anaesthetic to get something out of his eye. He did not know what was happening. He just knew that he had all that pain in his eye. His mother was holding him while the doctor was giving the anaesthetic and then proceeding to take whatever was causing the pain, out of the eye.

The boy looked up to the mother and seemed to say 'Why is this doctor doing this to me? Why is he giving me this injection and hurting me?' Without the anaesthetic of course, he cannot have the item removed and having it removed will cure all that is wrong with him. At the time, however, all the boy knows is that he is in terrible pain. He does not understand what is happening or why. The mother seems to be doing nothing to stop the doctor hurting him. Of course, the mother is going through the same agony and anguish as the boy.

That is a great picture of God when you are in a painful situation. You may feel that he has deserted you but of course He is there and is holding you in His arms. The pain, for a Christian, won't lead to death – because Jesus defeated death and even if a Christian dies physically it is only to live for ever with God.

Looking back now that story illustrates the pain and the hurt that I was feeling when I had just learnt about my illness. I cried until I had no tears left. I was also trying to cry quietly as I didn't want to wake anyone up. The sheer agony, hopelessness and fear of the situation drove me to tears.

It is hard to sum up where I am now. I believe that God, in answer to the many prayers for me, has used Rosalie Dickinson to bring me healing. I have had specific prayers for healing and I believe I have experienced healing, both physically and spiritually. While the experience in the summer of 1995 was anything but pleasant, I can now see good in it. It brought things to a head and helped me to get bits of my life sorted out and that might not otherwise have happened.

I don't know what will happen to me in the future but then neither does anyone else. The only thing that I have lost is the confidence I used to have in my health. At the moment my health seems to be back to normal and I try to live as normally as possible.

One thing I do have is a deep sense of gratitude every day for my health, strength and fitness, which before I just took for granted. I pray each day simply and sincerely, using the words of *Psalm 92*: 'It is good to say "Thank you" to the Lord, to sing praises to the God who is above all gods. Every morning tell Him, "Thank you for your kindness" and every evening rejoice in all His faithfulness.' I am so thankful to the Lord for my health but oh, how much more for the fact that Jesus died for me, to give me the certainty that I will live with Him for ever after I die!

13

WINNING THE BATTLE

The week the 1995–96 season was due to start with a home tie against St Mirren was probably the lowest I have been. I was struggling badly physically – at that time things still weren't showing any signs of improvement – and mentally I was totally concentrating on all the things I wasn't now able to do, especially train and play football.

I had missed my first pre-season preparation since coming to Aberdeen. While that may not seem significant to others, it was to me, as I had been on every Aberdeen tour starting with my first one in 1985. As soon as I had arrived, I had gone out to Solothurn in Switzerland with the first team, and further tours to Sweden, Holland, Devon and Cornwall, even Bermuda in 1991 and, more locally, the Highlands always got me ready for the months ahead. The buzz of the week leading up to the start of a new season is a highlight for any player, with expectations and hopes high.

Here I was totally down, and although not quite out, very low indeed. The high of the end of last season and the new contract was now a long way behind. The first match day was a very difficult day to get through. The team won well in the end, 3–1 against St Mirren in the second round of the League Cup, which was now known as the Coca-Cola Cup. As the teams warmed up I must admit I felt like going out on to the pitch and cheering and waving to the Dons fans. The meeting with the steward and the seed of hope was the one positive aspect of an otherwise discouraging day.

127

As the players trained, I was now walking. Day by day I was able to walk a little further and a little quicker, and the buzz in my back and legs gradually became less intense and lasted for a shorter period of time. The season got under way with a good start and I made a determined effort to follow the Dons as a fan and a radio commentator with the local radio station, Northsound. This meant that I wasn't watching with frustration at not being able to play, but could concentrate on the broadcasting aspects instead.

Initially after the public announcement of my condition I suffered a set-back and couldn't train at all. Then I started building it up. I tried to be positive. It has taken a lot of hard work. People used to say to me, 'Don't push yourself' and that would have been an easy option. But I knew that I had to push myself and not just stay within the comfort zone. It was important, of course, that I didn't do anything that would harm myself but I got the confidence from those who were helping me and advising me to go for it.

When you are told you've got MS, there is no cure and there is a good chance that it will recur at some time in the future, it is scary. You feel so helpless. But when the treatment started to help me and I was back training, it became easier to cope with as I was at least doing something positive. At no point did I feel my career was definitely over, but then again I knew of no one else who had been given the news I had received and had played again.

I was off and running by late August and into September. I was still getting the buzz in the lumbar area of my back and down the back of my legs, but once it settled I would then work in the gym to rebuild the weak muscles that hadn't been much used recently. John Sharp, one of the club physios, took me through the next stage of using the exercise bike and then more demanding stamina work around the track. I did three-minute runs, and five-minute runs with set distances. I was now fully into my own version of 'pre-season' training.

The team continued to do well, especially in the Coca-Cola Cup, where the signs were looking good for a possible trophy as the team beat Motherwell 2–1 after extra time to reach the semi-final against Rangers. By this stage I was reaching the possibility of making my own 'cup final' by playing my first game after the illness. John Sharp had done all the pre-season work I needed and now it was only left to take it one step further – a full-scale match.

On 17 October we were due to play Ross County in a match for the official opening of their new 1,200-seater stand. I was told that this was my target. It wasn't to be publicised and once again the press weren't aware of it until after the event. It was like getting ready to play in a cup final but without any of the hype. Just kicking a ball again felt funny. I tried to judge heading a ball coming through the air, aiming to regain the skills I had not used on the park for a few months.

The game was played and I was put on the bench. The photographers who were there realised they had some good material and were snapping at every kick I took in the warm-up for the match. I came on at half-time with the match well won by then, and after an emotional first touch I enjoyed the whole occasion immensely. To cap it all I scored a goal to complete the scoring in a 6–0 win.

Douglas and another friend, Brian Wilson, were at the match and they took me home afterwards. Once again the celebration was completed in a chip shop – this time in Dingwall – but it was Doug and Brian who had the late-night supper this time – I was content with a banana in a roll with mineral water. Again it was a great step forward with two special friends. We drove home from Dingwall happy and content. This time Brian and I really were having a good day!

Roy Aitken told the press after the match, 'It's great to see Brian back but I was never in any doubt. We expected him to return to competitive football and we've been proved right. It's a tribute to his professionalism and a reward for the dignity with which he has handled the situation.' I appreciated his comments.

After the Ross County game it was back to the routine of playing reserve games. This was the hard period. Having been part of the first team in the Ross County game, the next step, you might think, would be a full competitive game in the first team. Instead, however, it was back to the reserves. Fitness-wise I was feeling good. All the work I had done with John Sharp had made me ready to play. I also realised through this period that I had a good basic level of fitness and when my health was restored I was able to draw on the benefits of that underlying fitness that I had built up over many years.

John Sharp always told me that I would have no bother getting back to full fitness and he was proved right. But I have always been anxious about pre-season and obsessed with not going back overweight – all stemming I suppose from the bad experiences with Archie Knox in my first pre-season. So you can imagine how uptight I was this season, being so far behind the rest of the players as far as fitness was concerned.

It was obviously a euphoric time football-wise, and despite playing reserve games I was just enjoying being back on the park. The whole club received a boost the next week when we got through to the Coca-Cola Cup final, having beaten Rangers 2–1. However, the night of the semi-final found me sitting in my evening class for the HNC accounts course, having played in a reserve game against Partick Thistle earlier in the day. Although I enjoy the accounts course it was a poor second to where I would rather have been that night – playing against Rangers and enjoying the thrill of a semi-final win. It didn't help that the teacher kept going on about how boring this part of the course was. Talk about rubbing salt in the wounds!

The League Cup final came during the period that I was playing all these reserve games. I thought I had done enough to push my way into contention, although I knew it was unrealistic to hope to be in the starting line-up. John Inglis and Gary Smith had played in the heart of the defence all season and I wouldn't have expected – nor would I have wanted – one of them to have been left out for the final. In the end it came down to a choice of two from three for the places on the bench – Hugh Robertson, Scott Thompson and me. I felt that my experience might have given me the nod but in the end Roy felt that Hugh gave him added cover in midfield. Not for the first time I had to be content with a place in a cup final squad and a seat in the stand.

I watched the game from the stand, sitting next to Theo Snelders, who had been part of all Aberdeen's successes over the years and was now finding himself out of the team. We were able to encourage each other during a difficult season and I am delighted for Theo to be playing now at such a big club as Rangers, who seem to have taken the heart of the Dons defence throughout the years in Snelders, Robertson and Wright.

When Aberdeen beat Dundee in the 1995 Coca-Cola Cup final I was as pleased as any fan. But, from a playing point of view, I felt very disappointed to have missed out on a place on the bench. The bitter-sweet moments of the team winning delight me as a supporter, but at the same time you know that if they win you have very little chance of getting your place back. However, healthwise I've gone from the depths to the point of having my health back, so if ever I feel sorry for myself in relation to football, I just have to remember how great it is to be healthy.

One of the ways in which the trauma of the summer of 1995 affected me is that I now never take a game for granted. My preparation for every game is thorough but at the same time I'm not as tense as I used to be which is an advantage. I am now more relaxed about the build-up and it seems easier to go out and give it my best. By November I was fit but lacking the sharpness or match-fitness that only comes through playing first-team games. A few weeks after the final, though, I was unexpectedly put on the bench for the Kilmarnock game. John Inglis got a hamstring injury after an hour and I went on. The fans' reception was tremendous. They started cheering me when I was warming up. When I went on they gave me a real lift and once again that was worth its weight in gold.

After I had been on the field for two minutes, the ball broke to me and I laid it to Dean Windass in midfield and then I blacked out. For a split second I wondered what was happening to me. Then I realised that it wasn't just me but that the floodlights had failed. The funny thing was that the crowd went quiet and it was somehow very eerie. Dean, likewise, thought he had fainted.

I was picked for the game the following Saturday, against Motherwell which we won 1–0. Again I got a great reception. I was chosen as man of the match by the sponsors, which added to the day. Charlie Allan wrote in the *Evening Express*: 'It makes a change to be able to report some good news from a football match. Brian Irvine's return for the Dons was like a breath of fresh air in the current climate of on-field indiscretions and police investigations into matches. The Big Man showed no ill effects from his long lay-off and his battle against MS.'

The following midweek was the rearranged Kilmarnock game. Because of the abandonment of the previous game the club decided to let everyone in free, so we had a packed Pittodrie and a great atmosphere. In only my second game back I was playing in front of a full house at Pittodrie and we won 4–1.

An interesting question for the statisticians is, which was my comeback game? It was really the Kilmarnock game where I was on the park for two minutes before the floodlights failed. However, in the record books that game won't exist and my comeback will be the Motherwell game!

On the Saturday we played Hearts, my third game in eight days. Then because of Christmas and the bad weather we had about three weeks without a game. For the first game in the new year, John Inglis was picked and I was out again.

People were often asking me how I felt, and how fit I was. It is difficult to describe it really. I felt able to get through all the training sessions that the team did. I felt fit but also that I was getting fitter and stronger every game. It was, in a way, like having a wound that is beginning to heal but isn't yet back to normal, but with every passing day, week and month it heals further, and also goes further and further back in my mind.

May I ask the many readers who aren't Christians, what drives you away from God? Is it the misconceptions of him? When we see him as he really is, then we are not driven from him but instead are drawn towards him. *1 John 4:9* says, 'This is how God showed His love among us: He sent His one and only son into the world, that we might live through Him.' I am constantly aware in my walk with the Lord that I must keep looking up; the best is yet to come!

When I started writing this book, I wrote down, 'I have never captained Aberdeen. Along with winning the Championship, captaining Aberdeen is about the only ambition that I had which I have not fulfilled.' On Saturday, 2 March 1996, I fulfilled the first of the two remaining ambitions, captaining Aberdeen for the first time in a competitive match. It was one of the greatest moments in my life and it is hard to put into words the boost I received from leading the team out for the game against Kilmarnock. Roy only told me five minutes before the kick-off but I was on a high for the rest of the day. My dad was in the stand and he got the shock of his life when he saw me leading the team out! Around that time I also received a special award at the City of Aberdeen Sports Personality awards, acknowledging my fight back to fitness.

I captained the team in several games in Stewart McKimmie's absence. What made it even more special was that two of the games were against Hibernian, captained by Jim Leighton, and Kilmarnock, captained by Bobby Connor, two of my good friends in the game.

It got even better when the following week, in Stewart McKimmie's continued absence through injury, I was captain in the Scottish Cup quarter-final tie against my old home town team of Airdrie. It was a wet, windy and bitterly cold afternoon and Airdrie went ahead 1–0 to make us all think, 'Oh no, not one of those days!' Airdrie's great recent cup record certainly added to the worry. However, an equaliser settled us and with a replay looming Paul Bernard scored a last-minute winner to put us through to the semi-final, where we were to meet Hearts.

My run of matches as captain came to an abrupt end with a crushing 5–0 defeat by Celtic at Parkhead on April Fools' Day. It was an absolute nightmare and with the semi-final against Hearts as the next match, the timing could not have been worse. Brian Grant and I were the ones left out by the manager to add to the disappointment. From skipper to the stand – once again, what a difference a day makes!

The semi-final was a real disappointment. It was goalless for most of the game then Hearts scored. Duncan Shearer came off the bench to score a last-minute equaliser but Hearts grabbed a winner straight from the restart and we were out of the cup.

With only a handful of league matches left, I was a bit concerned for the remainder of the season. Disappointing, I thought, on two fronts. Firstly, the end of the season is one of my favourite times when I tend to play well. Secondly, after the terrible start to the season for me, the second half was shaping up well, with me playing regularly in the first team and with the real prospect of a fairytale ending in the Scottish Cup final.

However, the rearranged game from the semi-final date was against Partick Thistle a couple of days later and an achilles injury to Gary Smith opened the door for me to return immediately to the first team. Also, with Stewart McKimmie injured, I returned as skipper. Talk about a football roller-coaster! From 'skipper to stand' and a few days later 'stand to skipper'.

However, like my actual comeback earlier in the season against Kilmarnock, this match doesn't appear in the record book, because the Firhill floodlights failed to come on and with darkness coming down the match was abandoned after 35 minutes or so. But the fact I was back in the team made up for that disappointment and I kept my place for the next match against my old friend Alex McLeish's team, Motherwell, scoring the winning goal in the last few minutes as we clinched the match 2–1.

The game against Rangers in the penultimate league match at Ibrox was live on TV and the most important fixture of the season. It was to be Rangers' day as they won their eighth title on the trot, and Paul Gascoigne's day in particular as he scored a couple of great goals and a penalty to complete his hat-trick. However, we gave them a fright by playing some good football and, having just returned to the field after receiving stitches in a head wound, I scored the opening goal early in the match to silence the 46,000 partisan crowd. There were only 700 or so Dons fans so it was very intimidating but, to be honest, I love it when the atmosphere is so daunting.

What I didn't like was the behaviour of the Rangers fans who came out from a pub just along from Ibrox where they were celebrating, as our team bus stopped at traffic lights They proceeded to spit on the bus windows, throw their beer at the windows and, worst of all, threw the stones that thumped off the bus window. Fortunately the windows stood up to the impact but it left us wondering what the point of this violence was – and this was when they had just seen their team win the league.

The match was obviously big news in the UK with Gazza doing so well, and it meant that the goals were shown on national news at night. This was a tremendous opportunity for people far and wide to see that the Lord had made it possible for me to return to the field and that things were well. Many people who had heard at the beginning of the season about my illness would now have an opportunity to see me play and score.

When the league season had started I had gone to the Falkirk–Aberdeen match with Andrew Shinnie to watch the game while Andy commentated for Northsound. It was a bitter-sweet day. Returning to the scene of my first professional club, I saw the Dons win 3–2 to start the season in fine style, with a good attacking performance. As I sat watching, aware that many around me in the stands – press and fans – were thinking my career was in very real danger of being over, it was most disheartening.

But following the Rangers match our final league match was at Pittodrie against Falkirk and with Stewart McKimmie suspended I was again skipper. The match was an emotional high for me. I started the season by watching the Dons against Falkirk, whilst ill and seemingly written off, and ended it by captaining the Dons at Pittodrie to a 2–1 win against the same team to secure third place in the league. It was a wonderful day.

Once again I was last to leave the pitch, having waved to the fans all round the ground, thanking them for their support for the team and for myself throughout the season. I do hope that anyone reading this book, whether or not they have any faith in God, will see some of the 'moral of the story': never give up, for no matter how bad things may seem, they will improve.

My ideal fairytale would have been to have played for Scotland against England at Wembley in Euro 96 to end the season. More realistically, I would have loved to have played in the Scottish Cup final against Rangers which we just missed out on. But the Falkirk game was every bit as memorable and a fairytale ending to season 1995–96 for me, especially as I was skipper of the team.

Mum and dad were at the game, as were Joanne Dickinson and her son, Ashley, from the Tollhouse Therapy Centre, but Donna and the girls were on their annual holiday with Donna's mum and dad.

After the match I drove down with my parents, Joanne and Ashley, as I had the SFA coaching course to attend the following week before I set off on the West Highland Way walk with Doug later in May. Just like the previous year my end-of-season celebration was in a chip shop restaurant. On this occasion it was the Bervie Chippie in Inverbervie on our road south. No black pudding this time, but fish and chips to celebrate. Readers might think I am never out of a fish and chip shop! I am certainly giving good publicity to the chip shops that I've visited. The truth is that I stick to a pretty healthy diet throughout the year and enjoy a treat like this only occasionally, usually at the end of the season.

After the Rangers match, one of the things Gazza said made me think about something. He said the win with Rangers was better than his experiences in the World Cup in 1990 – when he really made a big name for himself! This sounds very hard to believe, because the standard of Scottish football is so much maligned that the comparison between winning the Scottish league and almost winning the World Cup (but for a penalty shoot-out defeat in the semi-final against Germany) seems to make Gazza's statement unreal.

Similarly, Doug Rougvie, at a sports forum I attended, was asked what his best footballing moment was. Easy, you might think – European Cup Winners' Cup final against Real Madrid in 1983, winning 2–1 after extra time. No! Doug had just won the Highland League with Huntly and felt that that was better!

These comments are not as strange as they may first appear to the reader. However, what they demonstrate is that today is more important than the past. Even lesser achievements become more meaningful when set against greater achievements which are diminished by the passage of time.

It also emphasises how temporary the ambitions and pleasures of life are for us all. Once an ambition is reached we need something else. It is never enough, as the ambition, once fulfilled and enjoyed for the moment, soon passes. The proverb that says two things are never satisfied in life – ambition and death – is relevant here (*Proverbs 27:20*). The one thing in life that is constant, that fulfils and never fails and above all lasts for ever, is a relationship with God through Jesus Christ as Lord and Saviour. As Paul wrote in the Bible, 'I press on toward the goal to win the prize for which God has called me heavenward in Christ Jesus' (*Philippians 3:14*).

This book was written and completed by the end of the 1995–96 season and as I look back from where I was to where I am now, I am truly thankful. In many ways it has been as good a season as any at my time with the Dons. I have a new lease of life and will appreciate it and enjoy it to the full.

My times are in God's hands. Faith can seem so straightforward, looking back, and seeing how things have worked out, whereas looking ahead faith can seem difficult as the events have still to happen. But God is great and as He has led so He will lead. My daughters, Hannah and Christina, trust me with childlike trust, a human father with all my weaknesses. How much more can we, as Christians, trust our perfect Heavenly Father.

A form of relaxation for me and, as you might recall, a help in my rehabilitation after the illness, was walking, and so at the end of the season 1995–96, after doing the SFA coaching course which I missed the previous year when illness struck, I set off with Doug, to do the West Highland Way walk – a 95-mile walk from Glasgow to Fort William, passing Loch Lomond and through Glencoe.

We decided (Doug somewhat reluctantly, as he is very camera-shy) to publicise the walk to help raise money for several charities, and this was something which I was thrilled to do. Others may prefer relaxation on a beach in the Mediterranean, but this is my way of relaxing – in beautiful, breathtaking scenery, lovely fresh air and away from it all. The great feeling you get at the end of a good day's walking is second to none.

The book has emphasised the truth behind the saying 'What a difference a day makes'. The greatest day and the most important by far was the day I trusted Jesus Christ as my Saviour and Lord. What a difference that day made! Through dying on the cross the Lord Jesus earned my salvation and by believing and putting my faith in Jesus I belong to the family of God for now and on into eternity. I believe that for every one of us the most important decision we ever have to make is to accept or reject the good news of Jesus Christ as our personal Saviour and Lord.

14

THE LIFE OF THE FOOTBALLER

When I speak at meetings people often ask me questions about the life of the professional footballer. From this it is obvious to me that there is a great deal of curiosity about what goes on behind the scenes at a football club. In this chapter I will attempt to answer some of those questions.

In a normal week without a midweek game, Aberdeen train four times, generally with a day off on Wednesdays. Training is for about two hours. During the season training is mainly practice, but sometimes, if the manager thinks your fitness needs topping up, you do a physical session on the Monday or Tuesday. I often try to do a bit extra with the ball after training under the Richard Donald Stand, as kicking the ball against the wall, heading it, passing it, and controlling it off the wall all help your game. By Thursday and Friday training is sharper, but at the same time shorter and less physically demanding. The emphasis is very much on practising match situations and looking at tactical points.

The canteen facilities at Pittodrie are excellent, with full and nutritious meals available for players after training. Part of the thinking is that with so many of the Aberdeen younger players being in digs, the club wants to make sure that they get a good meal! When Scotland played at Pittodrie, it was interesting to hear several of the players who are based in England saying that their club's facilities did not compare with those at Pittodrie.

If you have a midweek game on the Wednesday the programme is different. You train on Monday and have a very light session on the Tuesday, play the match on Wednesday, have the day off on Thursday and train on Friday. Aberdeen being where it is, every away game requires an overnight stay, so every second week we are away on Friday night. It is just part of the Aberdeen routine that you get used to.

The myth is that you only work 90 minutes a week, or, even if you count training, only about 12 to 14 hours per week. What is not counted is what you have to sacrifice to be in peak condition for the next match. This involves your whole lifestyle. You are restricted as to what you can do in the days coming up to a game. For example, many of our church social events are on a Friday night, which means that I can never go to them. Again, if you are playing away, you would not be home in time to do much on the Saturday evening. While I don't really mind that too much, Donna often gets frustrated that she either has to miss out on things or go alone. Diet is another important part of the training regime. I tend to eat what I want over the weekend but by Monday I am already thinking about the right diet in the build-up to Saturday. This includes meals which are high in carbohydrates two or three days before the game.

For a home game the tradition for Aberdeen always used to be to meet at the Ferryhill House Hotel at 12 noon for a pre-match meal and then go to the ground, watch *Football Focus* and so on. But that used to involve a lot of waiting around and the time could really drag. When Roy took over as manager the routine changed, and now we just report to the ground at 1.30 p.m. for a team meeting at 1.45 p.m.

The squad of 16 sit down and the team is named. Most players will know whether or not they are playing, but certainly there have been times when I have found out that I was not playing when I would have expected to play or vice-versa. Sometimes the manager might speak to you before the meeting and tell you. Personally I have always preferred to be told privately before the meeting. You are always built up for the game and when you hear that you are not playing you have this incredible feeling of anti-climax. The excitement on the faces of the other players just makes it worse. You have to hang around feeling like an unnecessary extra. At home games I usually go into the gym to work off the adrenalin and pent-up energy to avoid being further frustrated during the match.

After the team talk you go to the dressing-room, where the strips are laid out. I am usually number five so I usually have the same position in the dressing-room. Then everyone has their pre-match routine. I do things in the same way each week, not because I am superstitious but just because I feel comfortable with the routine and it helps me focus on the game.

By 2.30 p.m. we go out on the pitch. For the past three seasons we have done a group warm-up on the pitch. Then for ten or fifteen minutes you are free to warm up with the ball. I like to get the feel of the ball, practise some headers and so on. I feel that the warm-up is very important. As a big guy I need a bit of time to get loose and ready to play. I always fear that if I don't do it right, I could get caught out if I have to deal with a difficult ball early in the game. You have to be ready to start at 3 p.m., not 3.02 p.m. In addition your first touch, if it is good, can help you settle down quickly into a good game.

Then it is back to the changing-room. In the Aberdeen dressing-room there is always a lot of shaking of hands and wishing each other all the best. It is funny really that you have trained together all week and you might have played two matches together already that week, but from the handshakes you could think that we had never met or played together before. But it is all part of building up team spirit.

I always pray before a game because my relationship with God is part of my life. I don't pray to win but that I will play the game fairly and to the best of my ability, and that the outcome is the one that is meant to be. If that involves winning, that is great but for me how I play the game is more important. The idea of me praying at ten to three on a Saturday afternoon may seem strange to some people but it is perfectly natural for me. Christianity is not just about going to church on a Sunday. My Christian faith affects my life as much during the rest of the week as it does on a Sunday morning.

Then we line up and go out on to the pitch. Some players like to be last out or something but it never bothers me where I am in the line. Then it is on with the game.

For home matches we wear the club blazer and a tie when arriving at the ground. For away matches we always travel on the Friday in leisure tracksuits, and wear the club tracksuit on the match day.

For an away game, say against Rangers on a Saturday, we would report on the Friday at 2 p.m. and train for an hour and a half and then get on the coach at about 4 p.m. The tradition in Aberdeen is that you drive from Pittodrie to the West End and pick up the directors.

The coach journey passes with the help of videos. Since big Alex McLeish left, Duncan Shearer is in charge of supplying the videos, but his taste is dreadful! The record for the time taken before a film is switched off and replaced by another currently stands at one minute 45 seconds!

We arrive at the hotel – often the West Point at East Kilbride or one of the hotels at the airport at about 7.30 p.m. In the afternoon the physio, David Wylie, takes everyone's order for dinner and faxes it down to the hotel as it saves time on the night. I usually have something with pasta.

On away trips players always share rooms, usually with a regular room-mate. For years I shared with Stewart McKimmie, then at a time when his wife had just had a baby and he was having disturbed nights at home, he asked if he could have a single room. He assured me that that was the reason he wanted to have a single room, not because I snored or anything like that. Since then I either have a single room too or share with any player. Brian Grant has told me the boys draw straws and the short one rooms with me. I hope he is joking! After dinner we just relax for the rest of the evening and then go early to bed.

We used to do light training on the Saturday morning but then in about 1994 Eoin Jess picked up an injury training on the Saturday morning, so we stopped that. We have the pre-match meal at 12 noon.

Despite all the changes to our general diet during the week, most players are quite traditional, even a bit superstitious, about their pre-match meal. It is often scrambled egg on toast or beans on toast. I have tried a few variations but usually have something with pasta. Some players have poached eggs, cornflakes or plain chicken. Duncan Shearer will have a full cooked breakfast and then nothing more until after the game.

Duncan is the one who gives out the nicknames. He named Dean Windass 'Bungee' as he felt he must have done a bungee jump with the elastic too long and the smash on the ground left him with a flat face and nose! He himself is known as 'Benny-Five-Faces' due to the fact that he can talk very sincerely to one player about another, get the first player to say something like 'he's playing rubbish just now, I should be playing instead,' and then go to the second player and, putting on one of his other faces and using the information from his critic, get his side of the story.

When I was at Falkirk at the beginning of my career, I would often have steak as my pre-match meal. If it wasn't a team meal, my mum would make me a steak at home. Now, of course, we know that something heavy like a steak is about the worst thing you could have. It is also important to keep yourself topped up with fluids, so that there is no danger of dehydration during the game. Some people have special drinks but I really just stick to water – mineral water with the meal and plain water at other times. I will never get a contract for sports drinks as I never found that any of them did anything for me.

For an away game the team talk is always at the hotel and not at the ground. We aim to arrive at the ground just over an hour before the kick-off. Provided the ground isn't too far from the hotel, the physio will have gone over in the morning to lay out the kit so that it is ready for us when we arrive. We go down to the dressing-room, get changed and warm up ready for the game. When we play Rangers I am always aware of great hostility from the fans, even as you drive along the road to the stadium. During the game too there is the same hostility if a decision goes against Rangers. That hostility was never more evident than in the season when we went to Ibrox on the last day of the season with a chance to win the league. They seemed almost to be saying, 'What are you doing here? – and you'd better not dare to win or you won't get out alive!'

At half-time the traditional cup of tea is still what most players have. I usually have two spoonfuls of sugar in it because, psychologically at least, it makes me feel that I will have extra energy for the second half. In my experience managers don't throw cups of tea around the dressing-room at half-time, but I've seen all managers lose their rag a bit and Alex Ferguson was probably the worst. Archie Knox was another who would really let players have it at half-time. Roy Aitken is more calm and controlled in what he says at half-time, which I think is better. If I have had a bad first half, I need someone to build me up and encourage me for the second half, not shout at me and dent my confidence even more.

Players must accept criticism and be able to use it constructively, but how it is given is very important. A manager must know the player and make his comments in a way that will help the player to do better, not the reverse. With Scotland, whether it was Craig or Andy, half-time was almost another team talk as they tried to analyse how the game was going and make the necessary tactical adjustments to make the team play better.

Most years we play on Boxing Day. As a result, the players never have what most people would call a 'normal' Christmas. If we have an away game the normal routine is to meet at 2 p.m. For a Boxing Day match, the club will often put that back to 4 p.m. on Christmas Day so that the players can have most of the day with their families. After a bit of training it is off to the hotel, and after a snack it's up to our rooms where we spend Christmas night.

The routine is the same at New Year. As Aberdeen seem usually to be away on Boxing Day, we are then usually at home for the New Year's Day match, which means more time at home. However, as often as not, I will be in bed and asleep at midnight in preparation for the next day's match. That is part of the sacrifice that most supporters are probably not aware of. There are so many social activities that happen around Christmas and New Year that the player just has to miss out on.

Injury is an occupational hazard for the footballer. The set-up at Aberdeen is excellent with two physios, David Wylie and John Sharp. An injured player goes in from 9 a.m. to 4 p.m. for two sessions of treatment, either with the physio's hands or with the machines that are now available.

Aberdeen's facilities are now so good that it is very rare for the club to have to send an injured player to the Rehabilitation Centre at Lilleshall in England, something which in the past was much more common.

Being out of the team is hard. You are sitting in the stand as a fan, wanting the team to win, yet at the same time you know that if the team does win, you have little chance of getting back in the team. As a defender I am almost wanting the team to win 6–5, so that we get the three points but the defence has played so badly that I must have a chance of getting in.

The reserves are called the 'stiffs', and in the bus to an away reserve match there is a lot of moaning, especially among the more experienced players who may think that they are above playing for the reserve team.

If you are going to be a successful team you effectively need a squad which is so strong that there are two players competing for every place in the team. Sometimes the person you are competing with can be your best friend. I think it is so important that you find a way of coping with this so that you don't finish up thinking of a team-mate as an enemy. If you are not in the team you have to try to give your full support anyway. The thing about football is that everything can change so quickly. It is easy to think if you are out of the team that you won't play again. I have had times when everything has been going well then suddenly the manager changes the formation and my place no longer exists. I have felt really down about it at times, then the next week one of the defenders gets suspended or injured and I am straight back in again. If you keep working, your chance will come. However, if you don't handle it properly it can be destructive for you and for the team.

One aspect of football that sometimes annoys me is wage structures. Because clubs virtually never offer a player more money without being asked, it often comes down as much to negotiating skills and personality as to what you have done on the park. I certainly know of times when I have fared worse than other players because they have been able to sell themselves better than I have.

Usually it all works out in the end, though. Stewart McKimmie's experience was quite similar to mine. He was paid less than he deserved for a number of years but then got a well-earned testimonial. On the other hand there are players like Neil Simpson who was at Aberdeen for 12 years and left without having a testimonial.

I have medals from the various cup finals that I have been involved in with the club but they are not my only souvenirs. At Aberdeen you keep your shirt for any final for which you are in the squad. I must have ten shirts in the loft, just in bags. What else do you do with them? Some people frame them and put them on the wall but you can't put up ten shirts around the house! Not to mention my nine Scotland shirts . . .

A question I am sometimes asked is whether Aberdeen will ever again be able to compete with Rangers, who seem to have unlimited resources to spend on new players. With Rangers winning the league eight years in a row, the evidence would suggest that we can't. When Alex and Jocky built that great team in 1991–93 which came second to Rangers in all three competitions in one year and took them to the last game of the season in 1991, the gap wasn't that great. I don't want to sound defeatist but I think it will be even harder in future for Aberdeen to match Rangers (and Celtic) because of the money they have got to attract quality players from all over Europe. On the day we can beat them in the cup, but it is hard to see how the likes of Aberdeen, Hearts or Hibs etc could compete with Rangers and Celtic over a full league season.

When I signed for Aberdeen, they used to say that there was such strength in the squad that the Aberdeen reserve side was better than some Premier League teams. You couldn't say that now. In my second season with Aberdeen, we won the reserve league and that hasn't happened since. That was another tribute to Alex Ferguson's squad. The only way Aberdeen can compete with the big two is if the youth policy is right and we get our share of the young players. The club is talking about putting more emphasis on the youth side in future. I certainly hope it happens.

In the mid-1980s Aberdeen were the dominant team in Scotland, but Rangers were weak. I don't want to take anything away from that Aberdeen team, which won trophies that the later teams didn't. What I wonder, though, is how the 1980s Aberdeen team would have done against the present Rangers team, or indeed how successful the Aberdeen team of today would have been facing the competition that the team faced in the 1980s.

One of my disappointments with Aberdeen over the years has been our failure to make any impact in Europe. In 1983 Aberdeen won the Cup Winners' Cup and the following year lost in the semi-final, but after Alex Ferguson left the team was rebuilt and somehow never reached the same heights in Europe. Torino was the highlight of my time in Europe. We went to Italy and went 2–0 up, only to let them back into the game. Eventually they won 3–2 with a late goal. In the second leg we went ahead again to tie it up at 3–3 with us ahead on away goals. We let them equalise before half-time and they went on to win it in the second half.

If you look at the record of our matches in Europe there have been so many that we have lost by the odd goal or even on away goals. The record reads as follows: Feyenoord, 1987–88, away goals; Rapid Vienna, 1989–90, away goals; Legia Warsaw, 1990–91, 1–0 on aggregate; Skonto Riga, 1994–95, away goals.

The year we might have done something was the year we played Legia Warsaw. We lost 1–0, the goal coming in the 84th minute, in a game when we had our chances. Legia then progressed to the semi-final before losing to Manchester United. There is a very fine line between success and failure in any level of football, perhaps more so in Europe with the away goals rule. I can certainly think of a few games where we didn't get the breaks and didn't progress. On a different night it could all have been different. Who knows? If we had won the first round we might have gone all the way.

I am so grateful to the Aberdeen fans for all the encouragement that they have given me, never more so than recently. Alex and Willie were great favourites of the fans and it took me a while to establish myself with them. At first I might have been seen as someone who was taking the place of their heroes but in the end it all worked out great. I have already said how important encouragement is to me in building up my confidence and helping me to play well.

I have always had a good relationship with the fans and that is important to me. Scoring that penalty in the cup final obviously helped, although the season that we were nearly relegated also seemed to strengthen the bond with the supporters. It's now almost tangible. I love the Dons' fans and I hope they love me. Any respect they have for me is mutual.

I always try to take time to acknowledge anyone who wants to speak to me; if someone stops me in the street and wants a word, it doesn't cost me anything to stop and be polite.

You cannot describe the atmosphere in the Dundee United game – our last home game – at the end of the 1994–95 season. The fans were so much behind us as we were working together to keep Aberdeen in the Premier League. All through the week people in the street would say 'all the best for Saturday'. It was out of all proportion to a football match, being almost like a war-time spirit.

That support was special and it made an incredible contribution to the relegation fight. In the last games, at Falkirk and Dunfermline, their grounds were teeming with Aberdeen fans. We were all in it together. There was such a feeling of togetherness in the fight to keep the club in the top flight. There was one simple thing that I did which got a great reception. During the warm-up before one game I gave the fans in the Richard Donald Stand a gee-up, a sort of 'let's go' signal. Pittodrie just erupted and it carried on into the game. I made a point of doing it again before the Falkirk and Dunfermline games.

I sometimes feel that I am the fans' representative on the park. I'm a fan first and a player second. I suppose it is every fan's dream to play for the team and I'm the one who is living out that dream. When the fans chant my name I am bursting inside with such a feeling of happiness. I don't mean that it is a boost to my ego, rather a feeling of sheer joy.

I attend a lot of supporters' club functions but I never see it as a chore. I see it as a responsibility and a part of the job, but to be honest it is also something that I enjoy doing. I find that I never go to these events without getting something out of it myself. I hope, too, that I have given the fans their money's worth and that I have done my job well for them.

Loyalty to the club has always been high on my agenda. I have always seen myself as an employee of the club in the technical sense. I always try to respect the manager, even if I disagree with him, because I know that the club pays my wages. As a Christian too I believe what the Bible says: whatever we do, we should do it as if we were doing it for God. That applies to football as much as anything else.

The support I received from the fans during and since the illness was also incredible. Complete strangers stop me and tell me that they are with me. I cannot emphasize enough how this has helped my recovery.

15

GREAT PLAYERS I HAVE KNOWN

Throughout my career I have had the privilege of playing with and against many great players. At times in international football I have almost had to pinch myself to check that it was really happening and wasn't just a dream.

Over the years Aberdeen have had some great players. Bobby Connor is a real character. If he were any more laid-back, he'd fall asleep! He has a great wit and always had an answer to anything anyone said to him. His wife Ann used to give him a hard time, coming to all the games and telling him how he'd played. If he had a bad game, he'd be saying to you, 'First I get it in the neck from the manager, then I have to go home and face Ann as well!'

Bobby's name was once wrongly printed in the newspaper as 'Roger' and the name has stuck. Even his wife calls him 'Roger'. I remember a time when a player was telling story after story to the rest of us and getting on everybody's nerves with his non-stop chatter. Eventually 'Roger' said, 'Shut up, Stevie. You'd give an aspirin a headache!' I was on a coaching course with him in 1995 and had great fun with him all week.

Jim Bett probably had better vision than any player I've played with at Aberdeen, and he had a surprising turn of pace as well. I was saddened to see his time at Aberdeen end with him hardly getting a game in his last season, when I thought he still had a lot to offer. He always had great respect from the players for his ability, and he was one of the jokers of the dressing-room, a fact which may surprise some people.

Charlie Nicholas was another great character in the dressing-room. He kept the banter going all the time and when Davie Dodds was there too, no one was safe from the pair of them.

On his first day Davie Dodds was centre stage in the dressing-room, giving out stick left, right and centre. Willie, who always had his aftershave pinched by other players, got fed up buying expensive stuff just to have it used up in no time, and changed to a cheaper brand, one of the Brut range. Davie, not knowing the background, saw Willie putting some on after training, and slaughtered Willie for using Brut! No one in the Aberdeen dressing-room gave Willie stick, and here was Davie going for him on his first day at the club!

Hans Gillhaus had a great first season with us and got selected for the Dutch squad for the 1990 World Cup. Whether it was being with the Dutch team or what but he seemed homesick the next season, never produced the same form again and was away by the start of the following season. I never really felt that I got to know him. He seemed to stay very much in the company of the other Dutch players. However, he will be remembered by the Aberdeen fans for his all-action style and for the spectacular goals that he scored.

Eoin Jess, who left Aberdeen in early 1996 for Coventry City, is an exciting player. People think he is older than he is but he is only 23, having been in the first team since he was 17. He has tremendous ability. He will send a defender one way and then another with no apparent effort. Perhaps he never quite achieved what he should have for Aberdeen, given his ability. I think the best game he played for Aberdeen was a 4–1 win over Dunfermline when he scored all four goals. In 1990–91 he was scoring a lot of goals, notching 14 in all. Eoin is a local lad and despite all the media hype and adulation he has received, I have always found him a really down-to-earth lad. The big question for me is whether he can really fulfil all the potential everyone has been saying that he has.

Scott Booth is an exciting player in a different way. I know Scott's in-laws very well, and his mother-in-law, Margaret Robb, was someone I spent quite a bit of time with after the diagnosis of my illness. She was a great listener and helped me a lot during those difficult times.

On his day Scott can be as exciting a player as any you could wish to have in your team, and I have the highest regard for him. He has a great turn of pace and a real eye for goal. He has been hampered by a series of injuries, though, and as with Eoin the question is whether or not he can fulfil the great potential he has shown.

Gary Smith is a player I enjoy playing alongside as much as I did alongside Alex McLeish. I think Gary and I have a good understanding of each other and a great mutual respect, and we did well as a partnership. In the 1994–95 season when the team was struggling and I lost my place for a bit, it seemed to me that when Gary and I were playing together we were going well. When we were reunited for the run-in at the end of the season, I thought we created a solid base.

For a defender, Gary has amazing skill. Some people think he looks casual at times but I think he just never takes chances by trying anything he isn't capable of. He will take on a player because he knows he can beat him. He is quick and self-confident.

The best back-four unit that I played with was probably alongside Davie Robertson, Stewart McKimmie and Alex McLeish. When I got my first call-up for Scotland, I am sure that Andy Roxburgh was influenced by the fact that I was to play between Stewart and Alex, with whom I was used to playing as a unit.

Davie was very quick and would often use his pace to cover the rest of the defence if we got caught out. He had a great left foot and it was a big loss to the club when he moved on to Rangers. He had great maturity for such a young player, making his debut for the Dons as a 17 year-old against Hamilton in the game where I took over in goal from Jim Leighton.

Alex's record speaks for itself. He was the most thorough professional that I have ever played with. He worked hard to get the best out of himself and, inevitably, his attitude rubbed off on you and he brought the best out of you as well. He was just a natural leader. He was also a very caring person who would always take an interest in people and in their personal lives. He was a great team-mate on the park and a good friend to me off it. On many occasions I was out of the team because Alex was in, but that never stopped him giving me every encouragement. As a player I always had the highest regard for him and I am sure that he has the qualities to be a successful manager.

Stewart McKimmie completed the unit at right-back. He has been at Aberdeen for 13 years, and in his peak years he was exceptionally quick. While he is quite small, he will often outjump much bigger players at set pieces, but he does not score many goals, which the lads always give him a bit of stick about. Off the field he is a lovely, easy-going guy – most of the time – but on the park he can be very fiery. Behind us was Theo Snelders – but more on him later.

As a defender I am used to pitting my wits, skills and physique against some of the best strikers around. Mark Hateley was one of the most difficult opponents I have ever faced. Fortunately or unfortunately I often found myself up against him. He played in England, in Italy and for AS Monaco in the French league, but I think that he probably played his best football for Rangers, drawing on his wide experience.

I always enjoyed playing against Mark. He scored a lot of goals against Aberdeen but I always felt that I was still giving as good as I took. However, he had this annoying habit of scoring vital goals against us, and I would have to say that overall he probably came out on top in our encounters. In the early days he used to have a go at me but gradually I think we began to respect each other. It was always a tough, physical battle, but he was never a dirty player.

It is an accepted part of the game that you sometimes try to wind your opponent up so that they lose concentration and don't play so well. In one game Mark and I had quite a number of verbal exchanges and I thought I was just about coming out on top when Mark said, 'Brian, I've got more money than you'. I never did come up with an answer to that but I suppose it gave me an extra reason to stick close to him during games – he might give me some of it!

John Robertson is a tremendous striker whom I know from the Scotland squad. He is the type of player who isn't afraid to say, 'Well done, Brian' if you get to the ball before him.

Ally McCoist has the best record for scoring goals in the Scottish league. He is a guy with bundles of energy who can never keep still on or off the park. He is the type of player that you could keep quiet for 89 minutes, only for him to turn round and score the winning goal. Many people don't notice what a good player he is and the tremendous skill he possesses with both feet. That was something I became more aware of when we worked together in Scotland squads.

I played against Duncan Ferguson when he was at Dundee United. Even when he was very young he had so much self-confidence. I also remember playing with him for Scotland against Germany. He was so self-confident that it could have been just a friendly for Dundee United, instead of an international against the world champions!

If he applies himself I see no reason why he cannot become a big star. I feel at the moment, though, that behind all the hype he has still to prove himself at the highest level and to justify the superstar status that he likes to have. When he was in prison I dropped him a note, trying to encourage him. It was when I was ill myself and I remember saying in the note that the season had started badly for both of us and I hoped that when it ended we would both be doing a lot better.

I marked Ruud Gullit in the Scotland–Holland game. He was so quick and had so much skill that I just marvelled at him. However, what surprised me about him was how strong he was. On more than one occasion I got into the right position and got in the tackle expecting to win the ball, only to be pushed off it by his sheer physical strength. Thankfully you don't come up against a Ruud Gullit every week. I have not been in the least surprised by his success at Chelsea.

As a defender you are always very aware of the goalkeeper behind you, who is the last line of defence. The goalkeeper I have played in front of most times is Theo Snelders. I rate him really high. He lost his place in 1995, and what made it even harder for Theo was that he had been at Aberdeen for eight years – longer, I think, than any other overseas player in the league. Personally I will always be grateful to Theo for sending flowers to Donna and me when I was ill in 1995. It was a simple but sincere gesture that meant so much to Donna and me.

Theo has a strange sense of humour. On the coach home from a game, if a particular song comes on the radio he will tap on the table in time with the beat, just to annoy the boys. If everyone shouts, 'Shut up, Theo,' he is happy because he has got the response he wanted. In the hotel at dinner, he will run his finger round the inside of a glass to make a funny noise or pretend that there is a phone ringing. On the park, he can look like a robot, but there is another – fun – side to him too.

He took over from Jim Leighton who had been such a hero to the fans, but he soon won them round. I would argue that over the years

Theo's contribution of vital saves has been as important to the team as any forward's goals. And of course who can ever forget the penalty save in the 1990 cup final?

Jim Leighton is someone that I have stayed in touch with since he left Aberdeen. When we played Hibs in January 1996, I was on the bench. As we were going in at half-time, Jim made a point of catching up with me to ask how I was and said how glad he was to see me back. I really appreciated that. I remember reading in the paper that Jim said he had been devastated to hear that I had MS. The way he stopped me in the tunnel was a very special moment.

I have the utmost respect for Jim for the way he came back from the nightmare he had at Manchester United, when he was dropped for the FA Cup final replay in 1990. The nightmare didn't end there. If anything, it got worse at Dundee and I am just glad to see things working out for him at Hibernian. Apparently his departure from Manchester United was so sudden and unexpected that the United souvenir shop had 2,000 posters of him in stock. What do you do with 2,000 posters of a player who no longer plays for the team?

Bryan Gunn and I have had parallel careers. When I first came up to Aberdeen Bryan was there and he lived near me and often gave me lifts home. I played regularly with him in the Aberdeen reserves. Did either of us have any inkling that we would play together again in a few years time for the full Scotland team? He suffered a great personal tragedy through the loss of his daughter with leukaemia, but I am delighted for him that things have gone well at Norwich. He played well for Scotland and would have had an even better record if I had not stuck one past him in the Holland game!

Andy Goram is not the most athletic-looking of footballers but his agility and reflexes are second to none. Alan Hodgkinson's work with the Scotland goalkeepers has really done a great deal to improve the standard of goalkeeping in Scotland. The days when Jimmy Greaves can joke with Ian St John about Scottish goalkeepers are long gone. There is no goalkeeper I have played with or against whom I would put ahead of Andy Goram.

Chris Woods of Rangers was another excellent goalkeeper yet one against whom I often seemed to score. I think the problem he had with me was that I seemed to mis-hit some of my shots, like the one in Graham Roberts' last match so deceiving him. Despite my goals he was a very good goalkeeper when he was at Rangers and he holds the record for the longest period played without losing a goal.

Gary McAllister is a player I admire a great deal. It has been a great privilege to see him at close quarters training for Scotland. I first came across him when I was at Falkirk and he was at Motherwell, and he then moved to Leicester City at the end of that season before going on to Leeds United. There are so many different aspects of Gary's game. He has great skill and is a great leader, and he has been recognised in that respect by being captain of both Leeds and Scotland.

Paul McStay is a Celtic legend. He has done it all for Celtic and for his country. He has won over 70 caps for Scotland but when you meet him you would think that he had only two or three, he is so modest and unassuming.

The most difficult opponents I have faced are Roberto Baggio and Ruud Gullit. Unfortunately I am pretty certain that when their biographer asks them to name their most-feared opponents, the name of Brian Irvine will not be on their list!

16

MANAGERS

The manager of a football club is a key person. His role is to assemble the squad, to pick the team, to prepare and motivate the players, to decide the tactics and so on. If the team is successful, the manager gets the credit. If the team is not successful, as likely as not, the manager gets the sack.

Billy Lamont
My first manager in league football was Billy Lamont at Falkirk. Billy Lamont was more than just a football manager to me, and really looked after me in my early days in professional football. He even used to give me a lift to training. He gave me the best ever lift when he drove me to Dunblane to meet Alex Ferguson and to sign for the Dons.

Alex Ferguson
Alex Ferguson was the manager who signed me for Aberdeen from Falkirk. It was he who gave me my first chance in full-time professional football. He was immensely successful as manager of Aberdeen, winning league championships, Scottish Cups and League Cups as well as the European Cup Winners' Cup. Of course, he has carried on in the same vein with Manchester United.

Alex Ferguson was a very tough manager. I remember one game when the team beat Clydebank 4–1. It was 4–0 and Stewart McKimmie made a mistake to give away a goal. He fined the players all their win bonuses for letting in a sloppy goal. Another time when we played Rangers, two Rangers players were sent off and two Aberdeen players were booked for normal, run-of-the-mill fouls, but again both players were fined heavily for the bookings. That was an example of his tough approach to discipline.

He was the kind of manager that you feared and did not want to cross. It wasn't just fear, though, he also had the respect of everyone from the established internationals to the newest apprentice. Some managers try to rule by fear but don't have the respect and that doesn't work. Because Alex Ferguson had everyone's respect to start with, his tough approach was more acceptable.

He seems to me to have changed a bit at Manchester United. He had to earn the respect there as most of the players there didn't know much about him before he came. The fact that he was able to change his approach is just another indication of what a good manager he is. He is for me the greatest manager in the game today. His success, north and south of the border and abroad, is unrivalled. It is an honour to have been signed by Alex.

Willie Garner was the assistant manager at Aberdeen when I joined. He was only 30 and possibly too close to the players in age. Aberdeen won the league and cup double in 1985–86 but Alex Ferguson obviously felt that Willie wasn't doing the job the way it should be done and he was sacked. That was another example of Alex Ferguson's ruthlessness, and his willingness to make a tough decision for the good of the club.

Archie Knox, who had been assistant manager at Aberdeen before becoming manager of Dundee, now came back to Aberdeen. He was only there for three months, however, before he and Alex went off to Manchester United. While I don't bear him any ill-will, he is the only person I've ever worked under that I didn't feel comfortable with. I feel that he had a negative influence on my game rather than a positive one. He had a certain way of doing things, and although he was an excellent coach his style involved a lot of shouting at people. However, he had impressive records at Manchester United and now at Rangers and is obviously very good at his job.

158

I'll never forget my first experience of pre-season training under Archie in my first full season at Aberdeen. Pre-season training is always tough, and rightly so, but under Archie it was like being in the army. He seemed to delight in making it tough! I still remember going home terrified about what was to come the next day. Archie would joke that today was the starter and tomorrow you could look forward to the main courses as if today, with your legs rock solid and your body aching, wasn't hard enough.

I remember a reserve game at Stirling Albion where we lost 2–1, and Archie had a real go at every player in the team. At the end Brian Grant and I were together in the changing-room.

Archie was going on, 'This is terrible. That is terrible.' Then he turned to me and said, 'I don't know what you were doing before you came to Aberdeen but you should go back to it.' He told Brian Grant that he was just in his own little world, running up and down the pitch, doing nothing for the team.

I felt totally devastated by that. For the next week I went around like a zombie. That was the only point in my career that I thought seriously about giving up. The irony is that 11 years later, which club do Brian Grant and Brian Irvine (who 'had no future with Aberdeen' in 1985) now play for? Archie Knox would say that he just did it to motivate us, but you have to understand your players and know which ones need motivation and which ones just need more encouragement. I fall into the latter category.

What I did appreciate was that Alex Ferguson had a quiet word with me and admitted, 'Archie says a lot of things that he doesn't really mean. He does it just to motivate you. I know you've got your head down now but don't take it personally. I wouldn't have signed you if I didn't think you were good enough to make it.'

Ian Porterfield

Ian Porterfield became manager of Aberdeen in November 1986 when Alex Ferguson went to Manchester United. He was always on a loser. Alex Ferguson had brought so much success to the club that he was a very hard act to follow. Moreover, Ian wasn't familiar with the Scottish game. I feel too that he made a mistake in having Jimmy Mullen, who was also new to Scottish football, as his assistant.

His record wasn't bad. We lost in the Skol Cup final on penalties and the Scottish Cup after a third replay, and went out in Europe on away goals. While we didn't win anything, it was a pretty fine line between success and failure, but unfortunately he was on the wrong side of it.

It was Ian who was responsible for the signing of Charlie Nicholas from Arsenal. Like Jimmy Mullen, the players he signed – Peter Nicholas, Tom Jones, Keith Edwards and Gary Hackett – came from English teams. Gary was built up as a speedy, skilful winger. He got a great reception but by his second game he was not so popular. He never managed to convince the fans of his worth to the team and he was soon sold back to England.

Charlie was a great signing but somehow Ian never got the best out of him. When Alex Smith and Jocky Scott took over, they got him a lot fitter and his contribution improved a great deal. Charlie was not only a great player for Aberdeen on the pitch, but also in the dressing-room. He came with a reputation for liking the 'high life', but by the time he left he was married and settled with a family. So maybe Aberdeen was good for Charlie too.

For me personally, Ian Porterfield was great. When he took over I was languishing in the reserves. My confidence was low, due to Archie Knox syndrome! But Ian Porterfield played me and built up my confidence. I was, however, very disappointed to be left out of the team for the Skol Cup final, when I had played every round up to the final but now found myself 14th man, not even on the bench.

When Ian Porterfield left I was just about to get married. He still came to our wedding, which I am sure was hard for him having just resigned but I appreciated it.

Alex Smith and Jocky Scott

Alex Smith and Jocky Scott were joint managers of Aberdeen from 1988 to 1991. During their time in charge we won the Skol Cup in 1989, the Scottish Cup in 1990, lost in the final of the Skol Cup in 1988 and finished runners-up in the league three years running, culminating in the 1990–91 season where the championship was decided in the last game of the season.

t home with my family: Mum, Dad, Andy and Wendy

ndy and me in our Airdrie strips, ready for action

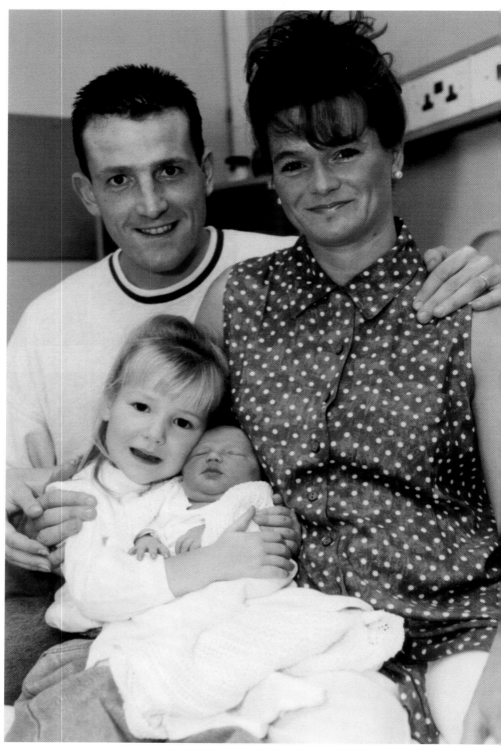

I spent the first part of my time in Aberdeen as a single man; now I am surrounded by girls

lly McCoist and Paul McStay make me feel welcome on my arrival at Hampden ollowing my call-up for the European Championship match against Romania

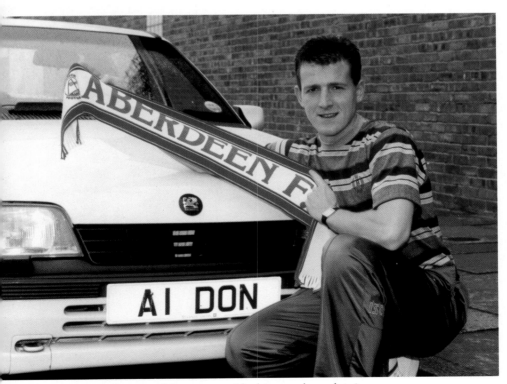

t has been my privilege to drive a car with this number plate!

2 March 1991: A late Hans Gillhaus goal which I helped to set up gave us a vital victo
against Rangers. Here I am surrounded by four determined Rangers play

6 April 1991: A 1–0 win against Celtic brought us even nearer to our dream of winning
the title. Unfortunately it was not to be

(ABOVE) Stewart
McKimmie, Theo Ten
Caat, Alex McLeish and
me, dressed to go to
Bermuda in July 1991 for
our pre-season tour

(RIGHT) At Arran, filming
A Day Out with Dana

Meeting Sir Cliff Richard after a concert at the Glasgow S.E.C.C. in October 1992. Sir Cliff is a wonderful ambassador for the Christian faith

Alex McLeish, Kriss Akabusi and me at a Duke of Edinburgh Awards presentation in 1992. Kriss is another great example of a Christian in the public eye

9 May 1993: Head-to-head with Rangers rival Mark Hateley in the Scottish Cup
match at Parkhead

Donna and me in the summer of 1995, hours after making the original press
announcement of the MS diagnosis

Gaining these Scotland caps was the highest honour I could ever have hoped to achieve

Alex Smith was appointed first and then Jocky was appointed as co-manager. That they are still friends after working together as managers says a lot about them as people. They were a great double-act. Alex was soft and Jocky was the hard man, although away from football they are both lovely people. Alex had the coaching theory, Jocky was more practical. They also had Drew Jarvie as assistant manager and his impact should not be underestimated. It was a good blend from the three of them.

Their success was well deserved and they put a lot into the club. The chemistry between them worked very well for a while, and it was when it stopped working that the problems arose between them. First Jocky quit and Alex tried to keep going on his own but ultimately he was sacked. Interestingly, they are both still involved in management but they never worked together again after Aberdeen.

One of the reasons they were successful was that their coaching methods were good. Jocky led all the training sessions, whilst Alex's involvement was more away from the training pitch. Alex was great with the young players – look at the emergence of Eoin Jess, Scott Booth, Steve Wright and Gary Smith. I'm sure they would all acknowledge the great help Alex was in their early careers.

Some people say that Alex and Jocky fell out over the tactics and team selection for the Rangers game at the end of the 1991 season. I am not convinced of the truth of that but it certainly seems to be true that after coming so close in that season, they were never quite the same force again.

One of the best things that they did for the club was signing the Dutch players like Hans Gillhaus and Theo Snelders. That was great when we were winning but the next season, when things weren't going so well, there tended to be a split in the camp with half the dressing-room speaking Dutch and the other half English.

Alex's end was a bit sad as the writing was on the wall for him, and, to be honest, in the dressing-room we were just waiting for him to be sacked. There were almost tears in his eyes the day he called the players together to tell them he was leaving.

On a personal note, Alex Smith included me in my first cup final when I was sub in the Skol Cup final, and I'm grateful for the chance he gave me. Again he picked me ahead of Willie Miller for the 1990 cup final and made it easier for me by telling me a week before the game that I would be playing. Of course, there were times when he left me out – like the league decider against Rangers in 1991 – but he was always prepared to explain why.

Willie Miller

Willie Miller was manager of Aberdeen from 1991 to February 1995. He was manager for three seasons and successful for two of them. He inherited a good squad from Alex and Jocky and he bought some good players like Duncan Shearer and Mixu Paatelainen, so he had under his command a group of experienced, quality players who were also committed. I think that helped him in the beginning as the team was easy to manage.

Another thing that has to be said is that worse teams have won the Scottish league than Willie Miller's Aberdeen. If we had not been up against such a strong Rangers side we would have won a great deal more. As it was, of course, we had all those runners-up slots.

Second was never enough for Willie. He was a winner when he was a player and he wasn't going to settle for second place as a manager. I agreed with what he was trying to do but many people felt that his way was too radical. He had a squad that was ageing but I felt that there were several players who left the club who still had a bit to offer, such as Jim Bett, Bobby Connor and Alex McLeish. Losing those three at the same time ripped the heart out of the team. The players he bought were good but they didn't have the experience of performing at the top level like the ones he let go. I thought that Willie never really got the best out of Eoin Jess and Scott Booth, partly because he didn't quite know whether to encourage them or shout at them to motivate them.

The team spirit in the last season was poor and Willie wasn't able to lift it. When the mood in the dressing-room was down, he couldn't get it back up again. The sad thing about his sacking is that the players were just waiting for it to happen.

There is no denying Willie's commitment to the club, but without the backing of the players he was never going to turn it around. Overall he had done well at Aberdeen. His commitment, more than anything, is what I will remember. I think the strain was intolerable for him in the last days. He cared so much about Aberdeen that the poor results really hurt. When I've met him since he seems so much brighter and not under the same pressure. I will always remember him as the best player I have ever seen playing for Aberdeen: a magnificent defender who did it all on the park.

Speaking personally, I always felt I had to prove myself to Willie. Even when I was playing regularly I still got the feeling that I had to play out of my skin to keep my place. That was great for my game, and so during this period I have Willie to thank for my consistent performances with the Dons which helped me get into the Scotland squad.

Roy Aitken

Roy is the youngest manager I have played under. Enthusiasm is one of his greatest gifts, and he has a tremendous attitude. As a player, he seemed never to miss a game. He was the main man in his team and a very competitive player, and the attitude that he had as a player has carried on into management.

Roy was in a no-lose situation when he took over. We were favourites for relegation. If we were relegated, no one would have blamed him but when we pulled through, he got the credit. Only time will tell how successful he can be. He brought in Tommy Craig at the start of the 1995–96 season and Tommy has lifted the tempo of training tremendously. Training is now done at match pace, which helps without a doubt come match day.

How well he did in keeping us in the Premier League and then winning the club's first trophy for five years! The same had happened in 1976. The Dons just avoided relegation and the following year won the League Cup, with goals by Drew Jarvie and Davie Robb. History certainly repeated itself very accurately. Following this early success Roy has signed a new three-year contract, and the signs are good that he will lead the Dons to the year 2000.

Andy Roxburgh

I will always be grateful to Andy Roxburgh for giving me my opportunity to play for Scotland. If it is possible, Andy is even more thorough in his preparation for matches than Craig Brown and he was always prepared to tell a player why he wasn't in the team. It is something that a manager does not have to do but a player always feels better when he does.

The game in Estonia was a good example of the thoroughness of Andy's preparation. He was a bit concerned about the facilities in Estonia and the hotel where we were staying, and as a result we took our own chef and all our own food. Because there was nothing to do in the hotel, he also arranged for a quiz with good prizes for the winning team. It all helped team spirit.

One of the secrets of Scotland's success over the years has been the great team spirit. There are no big stars, and everyone is treated the same. It is almost like the atmosphere at a club side. That is something Andy started and Craig carried on.

When we played Switzerland in what was Andy's last match in charge it was an emotional night. It was typical of the man that he should step down when he felt it was time for a change for the team, rather than clinging on to the job.

Shortly after the Switzerland game, I wrote to him to thank him for all he'd done for me and got this letter back:

Dear Brian,
Knowing Brian Irvine the football player has been a great pleasure – knowing Brian Irvine the man has been a joy. In football you meet all types because the game is not restricted to certain categories of people or social levels. I would find it impossible to think of any player I have worked with who has displayed sincerity, humility and wholeheartedness to a greater extent than you.

There is a short shelf life in international management and I am fortunate to have lasted longer than most. With the dawn of a new era for the Scotland team, I knew that change had to be made and it was time for me to let go. At the moment it feels like bereavement, but I am sure it will pass.

I shall watch your efforts with Aberdeen and Scotland with great interest. I can truthfully say that I am a fan of Brian Irvine.

If you ever need anything from me, please do not hesitate to call.

Kind regards, Yours sincerely, A Roxburgh

What a nice letter! I am delighted too that Andy has stayed in touch. I've had a Christmas card from him every year, and when he heard about my illness he got in touch again.

A lot of people think they are leaders when they are not. Andy Roxburgh and Craig were real leaders of men. The media portray people like Alex Ferguson as managerial giants, but I think that Andy and Craig are just the same, even though they are much less in the public eye.

Some of the players used to think that Andy was a bit over-the-top in his preparation and that there were too many meetings, but I appreciated it all and felt more confident in the matches because of all the preparation. Some people say that Andy was like a school teacher, treating the players like schoolboys. I have never agreed with that. I also think that the best way to judge Andy and Craig's relationships with the players is by the team spirit, and that's great at the moment. The record under Andy and Craig is pretty good too, encompassing qualification for the last two European Championships.

Craig Brown

Craig Brown has been great over the period of my illness, writing to me three times. He is a great believer in encouraging players and I certainly appreciate the encouraging words he has had for me.

Craig's great strength, like Andy's is the thoroughness of his preparation, perhaps helped by his background in teaching. No stone is left unturned, and he even asks players to stand in a certain way for the national anthem and not to chew gum during it. Match tickets for players are always taken care of.

Man management is another strength of Craig's, and he is very good at getting the best out of every player. He is very articulate and gets his points across well at team talks and meetings. He runs the training sessions and has brought in Premier League managers to help, such as Murdo MacLeod, Willie Miller, Tommy Burns and Alex McLeish. I am all in favour of this, and think it is an impotant strength to be able to admit that you don't know it all and to be willing to ask for help.

Craig always stresses to the players their responsibilities to the fans and the public. Players tend to see everything from their own point of view. Craig shows the players that they are representing the hopes of all the Scottish fans and sends us out to do it for them.

17

THE FUTURE

The way I view that future is that I am 'QC' – quietly confident in the Lord. I believe that if I trust God, He will look after the future. I don't want to be shouting my mouth off about things. I have just this quiet confidence, physically, mentally and spiritually.

The first time I was asked about the future was at the time when I started speaking publicly about my faith. Because football is such a short career, people start asking you very early on what you are going to do afterwards. As years have passed people have asked me less.

At first when I had just come out of the bank, I tended to say that I would probably return to banking or something financial. Certainly that was what Archie Knox thought I should have done – immediately, without waiting to see if I could make it in football! Then as my career went on and it was longer and longer since I had been in the bank, that seemed less likely. Also, as my career progressed it became all-consuming and I had very few thoughts about anything beyond just playing professional football. I had really no concerns about it.

When I was ill in the summer, in order not to waste any time, I enrolled in an HNC course in accounts at Aberdeen College, to refresh my mind of what I had learned from my banking qualification, and this was enjoyable.

The teacher, Alastair McColloch, is an ex-footballer who played in goal for Hamilton. He now supports Motherwell. We have great banter in the classroom and occasionally do some accounts work! My first game back was against Motherwell which we won 1–0. We also beat them 2–0 in the Scottish Cup but Alastair got his revenge when Motherwell beat us 1–0 in the league in February 1996. Part of the course involves computer work, and the next day my computer was dressed up in a Motherwell scarf and I had to take stick all afternoon. We were doing the accounts for 'Dougie Arnott plc' and 'Alex McLeish & Co' all afternoon! However, I got the last laugh when in the league match at Pittodrie we not only beat Motherwell 2–1 but guess who scored the winner? If you can't remember or don't know write to Alastair McColloch, Accounts Dept, Aberdeen College.

I have also done an SFA coaching course at Largs. I have done the B course and the introductory but still have my final assessment to do. At this stage these are just what you might call other strings to my bow. I am really just preparing for the time after I stop playing. In a way it is almost like your last year at school, when you are busy getting all your qualifications but are not quite sure what you are going to do afterwards. I am open to the idea of becoming a coach. I have always enjoyed working with boys. It is really rewarding to see a boy able to do something at the end of the session that he could not do at the beginning of it. As far as being a manager is concerned, however, that has never really been an ambition. I would be open, too, to some avenue of Christian work when I finish playing.

It has been great writing about my career with my beloved Dons and events on and off the park. I hope you have found it interesting to read of games and seasons gone by, family and friends, opponents and managers, but I hope, like me, the things you will remember most vividly are the most challenging parts in my life, such as when I became a Christian, when I was ill and when Aberdeen were nearly relegated. I have learned much in difficult times, especially on 19 June 1995 when the faith that I profess so openly became so real, and the theory became practice. The testimony I now offer of my Christian faith is powerfully given, but God's actions speak louder than words.

18

AS OTHERS SEE ME

Billy Lamont

My initial contact with Brian was as a trialist for Dumbarton while he was playing for Victoria Park Juveniles in Airdrie. Falkirk were obviously as impressed as Dumbarton were and had him signed before we could move.

Weeks later I was appointed manager of Falkirk and immediately put Brian in the first team in an effort to avoid relegation. We were successful and Brian became a permanent fixture in the first team.

In his time at Falkirk Brian was a colossus, both physically and mentally mature. He was a gentle giant with a strength of character matched by his fortitude and resilience, features which undoubtedly contributed to his recovery from illness which, in a lesser individual, would have had more serious consequences.

Ian Porterfield

As a person I rate Brian of the highest order. As a person he is disciplined and dedicated. He is very committed to his Christian beliefs but also totally committed to his football.

When I became manager of Aberdeen in 1986 he was on the fringe of the first team. When he was in the first team he never let me down. With Alex McLeish and Willie Miller at their peak, there were few chances for Brian in defence so I used to play him sometimes in midfield. I remember one game when he played against Dundee in the Skol Cup semi-final in a midfield role, marking John Brown (now with Rangers). Brian was magnificent that day and marked John out of the game and also managed to score the second goal in our 2–0 win.

Another game where he played a midfield role for me was against Rangers. I worked with him during the week on the role I wanted him to play. There were two things I wanted him to do: to lessen Graeme Souness's influence on the game and to mark Terry Butcher at set-pieces. He kept so close to Graeme that eventually Graeme lashed out at him and was sent off. Brian maintained his discipline and self-control throughout. While Terry Butcher did score for Rangers, Brian made amends with the equaliser.

As a person he was totally reliable. If you said, 'Training at 10 a.m.', he was there at 10 a.m. He is a great professional. The fastest I've ever seen him run was one Christmas Day that we were training. The moment training finished he was sprinting to the changing-rooms so that he could get to church.

When I was his manager he was still quite a raw talent but I felt that with good coaching he could become a very good player. It is no surprise to me that he has gone on to play for Scotland. And when he has done, he has let no one down.

Andy Roxburgh

'Ask not what your country can do for you – ask what you can do for your country.' Although these words were first spoken in 1961 by John F. Kennedy at his inaugural address, they retained their poignancy some thirty years later when Brian Irvine made his debut for Scotland. Few players in my time as national coach epitomised as he did the spirit of contribution and of dedication to the collective cause. Unquestionably the disease of 'me' infected some within the international squad but Brian, with his humility and his 'we' mentality, was a joy to work with and a valuable addition to the team.

For nearly eight years I selected national team players. During that period I worked with 70 top professionals and only one wrote to me to offer thanks for the opportunity to wear the precious dark blue jersey – Brian Irvine of Aberdeen. Brian never claimed to be amongst the élite of tartan technicians but in my book he was a superstar in terms of passion, enthusiasm and reliability. On occasions Scotland have been let down by big names with outrageously inflated egos. Brian, who got his chance with the international team because others were unavailable, had no such delusions of self-importance. For him the circumstances were irrelevant. Scotland needed him and he was willing to give his heart unconditionally to the team. The Brian Irvine I worked with displayed many of the qualities admired by Scottish supporters. He was brave, resilient, uncompromising and fiercely proud of his roots. His strength of character was a comfort to those around him.

There was a ritual in the Scottish dressing-room prior to every game. The players and backroom staff always exchanged handshakes and wished each other the best of luck. It was an important bonding and motivational activity. I could always tell by the handshake if a player was nervous or confident, strong or weak, excited or cynical. At ten minutes to eight, on the evening of September 12 1990, at Hampden Park, Glasgow, I shook the hand of Brian Irvine and knew that this was a player, and a man, of strong character. Brian made his international debut, Scotland beat Romania, and the first step to the 1992 European finals was taken. On that evening, Brian Irvine gave his hand and his heart to the Scottish international team. His was a hand worth shaking.

Craig Brown

There is much I could say about Brian but I shall focus on three main points:

1. Brian's willingness to visit our youngsters on 'Playball' and 'Goalgetter' courses. On occasion, I have asked him to travel as far as Peterhead and Fraserburgh to visit youngsters who are working on SFA courses. Invariably I included an SFA expenses form to enable him to claim for his petrol and other incidental expenses. Typical of Brian is the fact that he returned the form with a comment that he would not take any form of payment for visiting courses for youngsters. This is an uncommon, but highly respected, attitude to adopt. When with the youngsters, he is an outstanding example of not only a professional footballer, but a splendid person. His supportive

and courteous attitude makes him respected by youngsters and parents alike.

2. Brian's willingness to learn and to put something back into football is reflected by the fact that he has already embarked on his SFA coaching award. Having impressively completed his B (Basic) Licence diploma course he had enrolled for the introductory part of the A-Licence last summer when, unfortunately, he contracted his illness. I know it was a disappointment to him not to be able to continue but he has such personal resolve that, now that he has recovered, he is determined to continue with his coaching objectives. Early indications are that he would make an outstanding exponent.

3. In the international context Brian Irvine has never ever let Scotland down. Although somewhat maligned by certain members of the media, he has always given his best and been extremely diligent and responsive. Indeed, in my first match in temporary charge of the Scottish international team in October 1993 against Italy in Rome, I had no hesitation in selecting Brian to play against the impressive striking partnership of Casiraghi and Baggio. Although we lost the match 3–1, no fault could be attributed to Brian who had a solid performance against the might of Italy.

Brian's last game for Scotland (so far) coincided with Ruud Gullit's last game for Holland. This took place in Utrecht in May 1994 in a friendly match arranged to prepare the Dutch team for their World Cup visit to the USA in June. Again, although struggling for fitness after flying back all the way from Canada with an ankle injury to take part, Brian did his best against one of the world's superstars. Gullit was replaced at half-time but, before he left the field, he had given Brian a very demanding 45 minutes. To Brian's credit at no time did he resort to rough or ungentlemanly play which must have been a temptation against such an inspired opponent.

We are dealing here with an outstanding gentleman who just happens to be a professional footballer. I am sure that, in any walk of life, Brian Irvine would be a credit to his profession and, of course, to his beloved family. No praise is high enough for a guy who is one of the finest people I have come across in my 38 years in professional football.

Jocky Scott

My most lasting football memory of Brian Irvine will always be his penalty kick winner in the 1990 Scottish Cup final against Celtic. The penalty shoot-out had gone into 'sudden death' and Anton Rogan had just missed for Celtic. Next up for Aberdeen was Brian who was not one of our recognised penalty-takers. However, he stepped up to the ball and calmly side-footed the ball into one corner of the net with Pat Bonner diving the other way. A perfect penalty.

Brian is a commanding figure in central defence, has good ability in heading, good pace and good attitude, and is a totally committed and determined player. Over the last few years he has added good composure when defending to the list and at set plays he is always liable to score goals for his team.

It was no real surprise to me that he has gained caps for Scotland. In the season when he was first called up he was performing very well in a successful Aberdeen side. His form had earned him the chance.

Brian has great strength of character. He has had his successes in football but he has also had his share of disappointments. He has been left out of the team for a big game on more than one occasion. But no matter – when he was knocked down he has always bounced back.

Last summer he suffered the devastating news of his illness. You have to admire the way he handled that and came back, not just to fitness but to a regular place in the Aberdeen team. I have no doubt he will carry on playing for a long time yet.

Billy Stark

Brian was a valued friend and team-mate in my time at Aberdeen; off the park a polite, friendly, thoughtful gentleman, on it a ferocious competitor and true professional in every sense of the word.

When Brian signed for Aberdeen, my wife and I invited Brian for dinner one night. My wife had taught Brian at Airdrie Academy, and he proceeded to call her 'Mrs Stark' for the whole night.

I wish Brian every success in the future.

Alex Ferguson CBE

I remember well how and when I first met Brian. It was in the summer of 1986 and I first of all agreed the fee with Billy Lamont, Falkirk's manager at the time, at the Dunblane Hydro. I then went through to Brian's house in Airdrie, had a lovely chat with Brian and his father, and explained all the details about the transfer.

The part I always remember is how trusting he was and enthusiastic about coming to Aberdeen. I think these qualities have always been there and always will be. Later, on the drive to Aberdeen, I took to his lovely nature and manners and enjoyed the normally tedious drive – until I was booked for speeding in Forfar. I must have been carried away by the conversation! I have followed his career with great interest and he has been a credit to himself and his family. I was shocked to hear of his illness but also satisfied in the knowledge that he has great faith and determination and I am sure that will help him.

It was a pleasure to sign Brian for Aberdeen and a greater pleasure to have got to know him. I admire him greatly.

Willie Miller

The two words which for me sum up Brian Irvine are 'honesty' and 'commitment'. When I started in professional football loyalty and commitment to one club were much more common than they are today. Brian Irvine is a fine example of a player who is fully commit-ted to one club. He was first of all an Aberdeen supporter and from the day he signed for Aberdeen he never wanted to play for any other club.

When he signed for Aberdeen it was as cover for Alex McLeish and myself. To replace players like Alex and myself who have been in the team for years and who have built up a good relationship with the fans is never easy. Brian battled through, gained a place and did very well for Aberdeen and ultimately for Scotland. As a player his honesty and commitment shone through. He is basically a centre-half, yet was good at going forward and scored quite a few goals.

Alex Smith

My best memory of Brian has to be the winning penalty kick in the 1990 Scottish Cup final. During the penalty shoot-out, Brian kept getting further and further back in the queue to take the penalties. But when his turn came, he made a fine job of it.

A deeper memory of Brian would be his approach to his job and for that matter his approach to life. He had high principles and always set himself high standards. The way he conducted himself was an example to others. He was always ready to help anyone who wanted his help. In the last year he has had severe problems with his illness and has handled that very well.

In his early years at Aberdeen there was severe competition for a place in the team. He was up against two Aberdeen legends in Alex and Willie. That he played as many games as he did in the early years was a great compliment to his ability. Even when there wasn't a place for him as one of the centre-backs, he was so good that I was often trying to fit him in at full-back or even in a midfield role.

In September 1990 when Andy Roxburgh was struggling to find a replacement centre-half for his squad for the Romania game, I was delighted to suggest to him that Brian would be able to do the job for him. He got his chance and he handled it very well and Scotland won to get their European Championship campaign off to a good start.

At times in the dressing-room I would get angry with the team and use some colourful language. Brian never said anything but had a way of looking at me with a kind of scolding expression as if he was telling me off for my swearing!

Mark Hateley

When Rangers played Aberdeen Brian would always mark me. We are quite similar players in that we both rely on physical strength and heading was an important part of the game. Every time the two teams met it was the same story, one which could be described as a real clash of the giants.

It was always a battle. He was a very difficult guy to play against. Probably his greatest attributes were his strength and his heading ability. The size of his stature was matched by the size of his heart. He was very committed in his play and in his life. His commitment as a born-again Christian shows the character of the guy.

As a forward you tried different things to get the upper hand. Brian was always a very difficult person to ruffle. He was always very calm, and extremely strong. In short, he was always a difficult opponent.

Ally McCoist

One thing I have found playing against Brian is his honesty. He is a very hard and fair player. Even though I do not really know him off the field, the impression I get is that Brian is a proud and loyal person. His conduct is obviously very important to him on and off the field. I've had good battles with him in the past and look forward to a few more.

Bobby Connor

Brian is the only guy I know who hoovers his front grass. After he's cut it with a pair of scissors! His car is cleaner than Neil Simpson's used dinner plate. He has his hair cut more often than Stewart McKimmie argues with the fans (the Aberdeen fans, that is) and as any Dons fan will tell you, that is a hell of a lot.

Brian is single-handedly responsible for the disgustingly enormous profits of the northern electricity companies. Every time you visit his house you quickly notice that almost every conceivable electronic device ever invented is in operation – TVs, stereos, cookers, hairdryers, lights, lamps, microwaves, computers, shavers, curling tongs, the lot! You name it, it's on! And no one ever seems to be using any of them. They're just on. Working for no apparent reason.

One thing that sticks in my mind about Brian is that no matter where the team's destination, or the nature or the duration of the trip away, his luggage was always the same. A bag! A single bag! A shopping type bag, the sort used by the late Eric Morecambe. If you can recall Eric Morecambe in the flat cap, the long raincoat and scarf carrying the shopping bag then you can picture big Brian on a trip away with the Dons. The bag was quickly christened 'The Tardis'.

Whether a single overnight stop or a ten-day break, 'The Tardis' was the big man's only baggage. On arrival his room-mate would look in amazement as the big yin produced numerous suits, jackets, jumpers, trousers, T-shirts, magazines, sweeties, toiletries, dressing-gowns, pyjamas, slippers and so on and quickly filled the room's wardrobes and drawers from the seemingly ordinary shopping bag.

Alex McLeish swears he met Brian and his family at the airport one summer as they prepared to leave for a three-week holiday in Greece and 'The Tardis' was the only piece of luggage they had between them! Mind you, big Alex did say that it seemed to be bulging as never before and it had what appeared to be a flip flop sticking out at the top!

Football? He was quite good. Sometimes. Well, the odd time. No, really, he did have a good game once. I think. Maybe I read about it somewhere. He got a five in the *Sunday Mail*. Or was it a four? It could have been Brian Grant. He always gets a four. Anyway, who cares? The boy done good. Rightly so! Rightly so!

Signed: Robert Connor MBE OBE RSPCA and IOU

Stewart McKimmie

Brian's attitude is second to none. He plays to win and gives 100 per cent in every game. He is a winner. He is also one of a dying breed who needs no further motivation than the Aberdeen jersey. He has a real 'never say die' attitude on the field.

Brian is very realistic in his assessment of his own ability. I don't think he would mind me saying that he isn't one of the most skilful players who have ever lived. However, he plays to his strengths. His great assets are his tackling and his heading. He is a ball-winner. He is content to do what he does well, to win the ball and then lay it off to the 'flair' players and leave the clever stuff to them.

The other players really respect him for the sincerity of his Christian faith. As a result perhaps he does not get as much stick from the other players as I would in his position.

I shared a room with Brian for away games for several years. I've never met such a neat and tidy person. While I might take off my sweater and throw it on the floor in the hotel room, Brian would fold his up beautifully.

On a personal note, I admired how he has coped with the illness in the last year and how he has pushed himself to regain his fitness.

Eoin Jess

First of all he is just a very nice guy who goes out of his way to help people. When I moved down to Coventry City, he was the one who sent me a 'Best Wishes' card.

One of the first games I played for Aberdeen was a reserve game which was a kind of trial game for me. Brian was playing too. He tried to take me under his wing and told me just to play my own game. He still likes to remind me about this game and tells me it is all down to him that I got signed on! We still have a laugh about it.

He handled his illness very well and came though the experience with great courage. He was playing tremendously well when I left Aberdeen. That he was able to come back the way he did is an example of his overall spirit and strength.

Jim Leighton

Brian Irvine is honest and sincere, almost too nice to be a professional footballer. I remember an incident in training when he went down in the box and everyone was screaming 'penalty'. Brian got up and said, 'No, it wasn't a penalty, I just fell over.' I cannot think of anyone else who would have admitted it. He is as honest as that on and off the park.

I was with Brian at Aberdeen for three years. When he first came he was very quiet and shy as a person and quite naïve as a player. During those three years it was great to see him develop both personally and as a player. When I next played alongside Brian it was for Scotland.

I was really saddened to hear of his illness in 1995. You cannot say that anyone deserves an illness like MS but Brian was the last person you would have wished it on. It is great to see him back in the Aberdeen team again.

Roy Aitken

My knowledge of Brian Irvine is as an opponent, a team-mate and a player under my management. I look for three things in a player: professionalism, reliability and quality.

Brian is utterly professional in his approach to football, in his preparation for matches and in how he looks after himself. He is reliable and will always give his best for the team. That he has played nine times for Scotland is testimony to the quality of his play.

He has been a fine servant of Aberdeen Football Club. He is wholehearted and very honest. I can not fault him for the commitment that he has given to me and the club.

During the period of his illness he showed great mental and physical courage. While I hope that I supported him in this time, it was a very personal battle and a battle that he won. His courage was an example to many people.

STATISTICAL INFORMATION

Aberdeen FC season by season

1985–86	League	4th
	Skol Cup	winners
	Scottish Cup	winners
1986–87	League	4th
	Skol Cup	lost quarter-final
	Scottish Cup	lost round 3
1987–88	League	4th
	Skol Cup	lost final on penalties after 3–3 with Rangers
	Scottish Cup	lost semi-final
1988–89	League	2nd
	Skol Cup	lost final to Rangers 2–3
	Scottish Cup	lost round 4
1989–90	League	2nd
	Skol Cup	winners
	Scottish Cup	winners
1990–91	League	2nd
	Skol Cup	lost semi-final
	Scottish Cup	lost round 3

1991–92	League	6th
	Skol Cup	lost round 3
	Scottish Cup	lost round 3
1992–93	League	2nd
	Skol Cup	lost final to Rangers 1–2
	Scottish Cup	lost final to Rangers 1–2
1993–94	League	2nd
	Skol Cup	lost quarter-final
	Scottish Cup	lost semi-final replay
1994–95	League	9th
	Coca-Cola Cup	lost semi-final
	Scottish Cup	lost round 4
1995–96	League	3rd
	Coca-Cola Cup	winners
	Scottish Cup	lost semi-final

Brian Irvine: Falkirk playing record

	League	League Cup	Scottish Cup	Friendly	Total
1983–84	3	–	–	–	3
1984–85	35	1	2	3	41
Total	38	1	2	3	44

No goals for Falkirk

Brian Irvine: Aberdeen playing record

	League	League Cup	Scottish Cup	European	Friendly	**Total**
1985–86	1	–	–	–	8	9
1986–87	20	2	–	1	7	30
1987–88	17	4	1	1	4	27
1988–89	27	3	5	1	5	41
1989–90	31	3	5	1	2	42
1990–91	30	4	1	4	7	46
1991–92	41	2	1	2	5	51
1992–93	39	3	6	–	5	53
1993–94	42	2	6	4	5	59
1994–95	19	2	1	2	3	27
1995–96	18	–	3	–	2	23
Total	285	25	29	16	53	408

Not included:

30 games as unused substitute

4 abandoned games

Brian Irvine: Aberdeen scoring record

30 Jul 1985	F	Lausanne, Switzerland	A	6–2
27 Jul 1986	F	Vara Select, Sweden	A	3–0
14 Mar 1987	L	Celtic	H	1–0
11 Apr 1987	L	Clydebank	H	1–1
2 May 1987	L	Rangers	H	1–1
19 Aug 1987	LC	Brechin City	H	5–1
23 Sep 1987	LC	Dundee	N	2–0
30 Apr 1988	L	Rangers	A	1–0
17 Dec 1988	L	St Mirren	H	3–1
25 Feb 1989	L	Hearts	H	3–0
17 Mar 1990	SC	Hearts	H	4–1
14 Apr 1990	SC	Dundee United	N	4–0
28 Apr 1990	L	St Mirren	H	2–0
9 May 1990	SC	Celtic	N	9–8
29 Aug 1990	LC	Stranraer	H	4–0
22 Sep 1990	L	St Mirren	H	2–1
15 Dec 1990	L	Dunfermline	H	3–2
10 Aug 1991	L	Airdrie	A	2–1
5 Oct 1991	L	St Mirren	H	4–1
4 Dec 1991	L	Rangers	H	2–3
28 Mar 1992	L	Airdrie	H	1–0
25 Aug 1992	LC	Falkirk	A	4–1
28 Nov 1992	L	Hearts	H	6–2
5 Dec 1992	L	St Johnstone	H	3–0
12 Dec 1992	L	Dundee United	A	2–2
26 Dec 1992	L	Motherwell	A	2–0
9 Jan 1993	SC	Hamilton	H	4–1
16 Jan 1993	L	Airdrie	H	7–0
16 Mar 1993	SC	Clydebank	A	4–3
29 Sep 1993	ECWC	Valur, Iceland	H	4–0
14 Dec 1993	L	Partick Thistle	H	2–1
11 Jan 1994	L	Dundee	A	1–0
19 Jan 1994	L	Celtic	A	2–2
27 Apr 1994	L	Hearts	A	1–1
30 Apr 1994	L	Dundee	H	1–1

7 May 1994	L	St Johnstone	A	1–0
14 May 1994	L	Celtic	H	1–1
15 Apr 1995	L	Celtic	H	2–0
17 Oct 1995	F	Ross County	A	6–0
23 Jan 1996	L	Kilmarnock	A	1–1
13 Apr 1996	L	Motherwell	H	2–1
27 Apr 1996	L	Rangers	A	1–3
11 May 1996	F	Isle of Lewis	A	6–0

F – Friendly
L – League
LC – League Cup
SC – Scottish Cup
ECWC – European Cup Winners' Cup

A – Away
H – Home
N – Neutral

Brian Irvine: international caps

	World Cup Qualifier	European Champs Qualifier	Friendly	Total
1990–91	–	1	–	1
1991–92	–	–	–	–
1992–93	2	–	1	3
1993–94	3	–	2	5

12 September 1990 Scotland 2 Romania 1 (European Championship) Hampden Park

24 March 1993 Scotland 0 Germany 1 (Friendly), Ibrox

19 May 1993 Estonia 0 Scotland 3 (World Cup Qualifier), Tallin

2 June 1993 Scotland 3 Estonia 1 (World Cup Qualifier), Aberdeen

8 September 1993 Scotland 1 Switzerland 1 (World Cup Qualifier), Aberdeen

13 October 1993 Italy 3 Scotland 1 (World Cup Qualifier), Rome

17 November 1993 Malta 0 Scotland 2 (World Cup Qualifier), Ta Quali

20 April 1994 Austria 1 Scotland 2 (Friendly), Vienna

27 May 1994 Holland 3 Scotland 1 (Friendly), Utrecht

Non-playing member of Scotland squad:
Switzerland 1990
Holland   1993
Portugal   1993
Finland   1994

INDEX

187

Germany 25, 48
Gilfeather, Frank 114–15
Gill, Jim 41
Gillhaus, Hans 51, 52, 68, 150, 161
Gilmour's groin 72–73
Glass, Steve 103, 104
Goalkeeper, Brian Irvine as 33, 79
Goals (by Brian Irvine) 35, 36, 39, 41, 48, 51, 71, 78, 85, 93–94, 100, 129, 134, 135
God 13, 23, 37, 41, 42, 46, 54, 70, 79, 87, 88, 100, 109, 110, 111, 115, 118, 121, 122, 124, 132, 134, 135, 136, 137, 140, 148, 167, 168
Goram, Andy 79, 86, 154
Gough, Richard 56, 60
Graham, Billy 73, 79, 102
Grant, Brian 31, 51, 52, 97, 101, 133, 142, 159, 177
Gray, Derek 115
Green Final 60
Gullit, Ruud 44, 64, 65, 153, 155, 172
Gunn, Bryan 62, 154

Hackett, Gary 160
Hamilton Academicals 22, 85, 151
Hanover 48
Harper, Joe 16
Hateley, Mark 85, 86, 152, 175–76
Hearts 12, 33, 35, 39, 48, 68, 79, 84, 85, 92, 93, 100, 101, 103, 132, 133, 146
Herd, Graham 105

Hetherston, Peter 17, 95
Hibernian 12, 33, 39, 78, 79, 85, 92, 99, 101, 146, 154
Holland 44, 63, 64, 89, 92, 172
Hughes, John 18
Hughes, Mark 76

Inglis, John 95–96, 98, 100, 130, 131
Inverness Caley 31
Irvine, Andrew 15, 17
Irvine, Bill and Isobel 15, 16, 35–36, 135
Irvine, Christina 45, 98, 123
Irvine, Donna 11, 12, 34–36, 40, 45, 46, 54, 58, 80, 81, 87, 98, 100, 101, 103, 106, 108, 109, 113, 114, 117, 118, 120, 123, 135, 140, 153
Irvine, Hannah 45, 68, 81, 123
Irvine, Hazel 102
Irvine, Wendy 15
Italy 91, 172

Jarvie, Drew 16, 161, 163
Jess, Eoin 42, 43, 79, 85, 91, 102, 142, 150, 161–62, 178
Jesus 13, 22, 23, 88, 112, 125, 136, 137
Jones, Tom 160

Kane, Paul 97
Kennedy, John F. 170
Kilmarnock 12, 19, 57, 99, 131, 132, 133
Kintore Parish Church 29, 30, 35, 49
Kirk, Stevie 24